EVERYMAN,
I WILL GO WITH THEE
AND BE THY GUIDE,
IN THY MOST NEED
TO GO BY THY SIDE

EVERYMAN'S LIBRARY
POCKET POETS

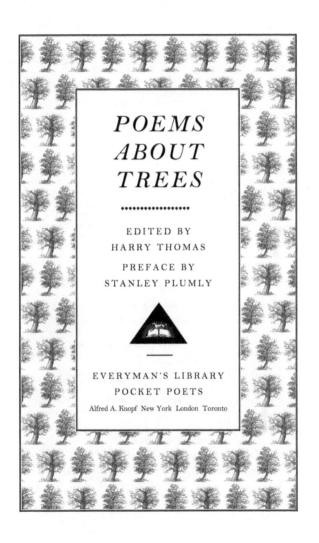

POEMS ABOUT TREES

EDITED BY
HARRY THOMAS

PREFACE BY
STANLEY PLUMLY

EVERYMAN'S LIBRARY
POCKET POETS

Alfred A. Knopf New York London Toronto

THIS IS A BORZOI BOOK

PUBLISHED BY ALFRED A. KNOPF

This selection by Harry Thomas first published in
Everyman's Library, 2019
Copyright © 2019 by Everyman's Library

Fourth printing (US)

A list of acknowledgments to copyright owners appears at the back
of this volume.

www.randomhouse.com/everymans
www.everymanslibrary.co.uk

ISBN 978-1-101-90815-0 (US)
978-1-84159-817-8 (UK)

A CIP catalogue record for this book is available from the British Library

Library of Congress Cataloging-in-Publication Data

Names: Thomas, Harry, 1952– editor.
Title: Poems about trees / edited by Harry Thomas.
Description: New York: Alfred A. Knopf [2019] | Series: Everyman's library
pocket poets series
Identifiers: LCCN 2019013640 | ISBN 9781101908150 (hardback)
Subjects: LCSH: Trees—Poetry. | BISAC: POETRY/Anthologies
(multiple authors).
Classification: LCC PN6110.T75 P58 2019 | DDC 808.81/9364—dc23
LC record available at https://lccn.loc.gov/2019013640

Typography by Peter B. Willberg

Typeset in the UK by Input Data Services Ltd, Isle Abbotts, Somerset

Printed and bound in Germany by GGP Media GmbH, Pössneck

CONTENTS

PLANTING AND PRESERVING

GROVE, WOODS, ORCHARD, FOREST

PREFACE

Harry Thomas has arranged his anthology of tree poems as much around complex attitudes toward trees as dramatic evocations of their arboreal being: ranging from the "gladness" of the fact of them to their natural, named, and significant presences to – sadly but beautifully – their "gladness gone." Which is to say Thomas' selection is emotional as well as analytical, political as well as philosophical, as it moves from celebration to meditation, from the reality and imagination of what trees are to a deepening awareness of what their loss means.

The range of poets is equally rich in variety, nationality, and history. Though the overall emphasis may be Anglo-American and the living moment especially contemporaneous, the individual poems develop in perspective from Homer's *Odyssey* and Virgil's *Georgics* to examples from Matsuo Basho and Yosa Buson to any number of international figures such as Eugenio Montale, Czeslaw Milosz, Bertolt Brecht, Giorgio Bassani, and Nuala Ni Dhomhnaill, in first-rate translations by Lee Gerlach, Robert Hass, Edwin Morgan, Jamie McKendrick, and Paul Muldoon. Indeed, "From all these trees,/in the salads, the soup, everywhere,/cherry blossoms fall" – writes the seventeenth-century Japanese poet Basho in the Hass version.

11

The mixture of tradition, innovation, and generation is as exciting as it is informing. You cannot assemble a tree anthology of poems without such classics as Wordsworth's "Nutting" or Housman's "Loveliest of Trees" or Whitman's "I Saw in Louisiana a Live-Oak Growing" or Marianne Moore's "The Camperdown Elm." You cannot test the quality of the originality of the poetry without Montale's "The Lemon Trees" or Seamus Heaney's "The Birch Grove" or Rainer Maria Rilke's "The Apple Orchard" (translated by Seamus Heaney). You cannot include the present without pairing such poems as Mary Oliver's "The Black Walnut Tree" with Ellen Bryant Voigt's "Landscape, Dense with Trees" or Judith Wright's lyrical "Train Journey" with her massive meditation "The Cedars" or James Wright's elegiac "To a Blossoming Pear Tree" with Marvin Bell's lovely lament "These Green-Going-to-Yellow."

In terms of tone and poetic temperament, Thomas has effectively exercised his editorial rights to choices that are not only carefully crafted but open-ended in form and ambition; he values discipline and understatement but at the same time admires "tree" poems that think with their hearts, that enlarge the view with vision. David Ferry's "Everybody's Tree" is just that kind of contemporary visionary poem that at some one hundred associative, narrative lines, structured in moments like paragraphs, develops around both personal history and the larger caring time of local community, in a voice at once filled with losses and empathy for those losses. And no poet could be more empathic and expansive than Keats-contemporary John Clare in his "sweetest anthem" "To a Fallen Elm" – its wide, searching lines of direct address may come close to anger but they also abide with love.

There is so much to admire here in this beautifully focused gathering of poems, both in the familiar and as discovery. Some of my own favorites are Wordsworth's "Yew Trees," W. C. Williams' "Burning the Christmas Greens," Jorie Graham's "Tree Surgeons," Robert Graves' "Not Dead," Gerald Stern's "The Cemetery of Orange Trees in Crete," James Dickey's "In the Tree House at Night," and on and on. Because Thomas has arranged his selections around centers of both generosity and gravity he never loses sight of the essential thing: that trees are the great flowers of our world – life-givers, life-enhancers, life-poetry. They literally stand at the line between life and death. How many kinds of trees are there, how many purposes, how many differences among the domestic and the wild, the old growth and the new, the abrupt edges and the farmer's field?

We love trees for a reason, we cut them down for other reasons, we kill them at our peril. The Ojebway believe that cutting down living trees is like the wounding and killing of animals. The pointless downing of trees is probably worse. For many decades my family's business was the harvesting of trees, a business that would often take my father and his crews out into the Shenandoah for days at a time. This was in the Forties, during and after the war. As a small boy I'd sometimes go out with the men for a couple of days, if for nothing else than the feeling of being among the looming hardwoods – the big white oaks and scarlet and silver maples and shagbark hickories and massive black walnuts. Just to try to look straight up among them would be to lose your balance, yet their very presences changed the sky and lifted it all somehow.

The man-made cutting and trimming was one thing. The other was the natural competition for sunlight and rain and space among the trees themselves, so that there was an inevitable wear and tear and rot and fall that would leave the forest floor covered with ruins, all mixed up in layers of branch and root and debris. Such places in the woods always struck me as sad yet also sacred places, since, when I was old enough to really think about it, they were in-between places where the trees had decided the difference between the past and the future.

Stanley Plumly

INTRODUCTION

The oldest trees still in the world and the poetic record of living among trees go back to almost the same ancient time. The oldest tree is the bristlecone pine that grows in sparse groves on slopes high (10,000–11,000 feet) in the White Mountains of California and Nevada. For years Methuselah was known as the single oldest tree, being over 4,800 years old, but recently a tree near it was found to have lived longer than 5,000 years. Both these bristlecone pines then were beginning to establish themselves in the hard dolomite rock of the mountains when the first ballads about Gilgamesh were likely being sung in Mesopotamia. In the Standard Version of the Gilgamesh epic, set down two thousand years later, when Methuselah and its neighbor were about midpoint in their span of life, the first adventure that Gilgamesh and Enkidu, his friend and companion, undertake is to travel a long way to the vast Cedar Forest in what is now Syria. Their aim is to kill Huwawa, the Guardian of the Forest, who was appointed to the office by the gods who dwell in the trees, to cut down the cedars, and float them back to be milled in their city. Even so, the Babylonian poet or poets who wrote the epic were aware of what was being lost: "Beautiful is the forest; green upon green the cedars; fragrant the air with the fragrance of the cedar trees." Much of what we have experienced and are still experiencing with trees, their beauty, their fragrance, their sustaining clean air, and their disappearance under axe or saw, is depicted in this part of the ancient poem.

I've included no passage from *Gilgamesh* in this book, but I have chosen two passages from the *Odyssey*, because at several points trees play a crucial role in that epic. Two instances: the recognition scenes at the end depend on trees. Odysseus convinces Penelope that he is in fact her husband by describing how he constructed their bed from an olive tree growing in the middle of their bedroom, and to his aged father, who is tending his orchard when Odysseus comes to find him, he proves his identity by recalling how as a boy he begged his father to plant an orchard for him: "you named them one by one. You gave me thirteen pear, ten apple trees and forty figs." We feel Odysseus's lifelong excitement at being among the family fruit trees, a fact never commented on, as far as I know, in discussions of the guileful hero. The tree-loving side of the character comes across best in a passage in Book 6, when, emerging from the double olive thicket where he has spent the night, Odysseus encounters Nausicaa, the princess of the island where he has been shipwrecked. He needs her help, and at first his speech expresses that need, but then he is swept away by her beauty, telling her that he has never before seen such beauty, unless it was

> in Delos, beside Apollo's altar –
> the young slip of a palm-tree springing into the
>   light ...
> That vision! Just as I stood there gazing, rapt, for
>   hours ...
> no shaft like that had ever risen up from the
>   earth –

The reader may feel as I do that this is an extra-ordinary moment in the history of poetry, and one that uncannily looks ahead to moments of visionary glad-ness in Anglo-American poetry since Wordsworth. Indeed, the first section of this anthology, which I've called "Gladness," contains many poems that seem to have been inspired, unlikely as that is, by the passage I've just quoted from the *Odyssey*. The poems are by Wordsworth, Edward Thomas, Gerard Manley Hop-kins, two poetic prose pieces by Emerson and Thoreau, Yves Bonnefoy, and others. James Dickey speaks of his being "in holy alliance" with a tree that "leaps up on wings that could save me from death." It was my first desire in making this book to present passages such as this one to demonstrate that animism, the heart of which was a reverence, at times ecstatic, for the "holy alliance" between humans and trees, lives on in modern and contemporary poetry.

Surely it is the feeling of spiritual fellowship with

trees, and sometimes, as in Stanley Plumly's "Panegyric for the Plane Tree Fallen on Fifth Avenue," one tree, that accounts for our heartache at their loss. Trees perish from many causes — floods, fires, hurricanes, tornadoes, lightning, ice-storms, storms of lashing wind and driving rain, insect infestation, disease. In Watertown, Massachusetts, we lost the hundred-year-old birch tree that grew just outside our house because we weren't there to shake the branches during a heavy ice-storm. When we arrived home we found that the trunk of the tree had been split in two and the crown lay on the grass. I felt remiss, and hurt.

But the poets in "Gladness Gone" write of feeling worse than hurt when trees they love are deliberately, suddenly felled. Hopkins was for some time inconsolable after he discovered one day that the double row of aspens on the river bank, trees he had been in the habit of walking to see since his arrival at Oxford, had all been felled, "not spared, not one," in order to make brake shoes for the Great Western Railway. The loss was irremediable, but that day he wrote "Binsey Poplars." Similarly, Thoreau, in *Walden*, decried the cutting down for firewood of the trees along the shore of the lake. "How can you expect the birds to sing when their groves are cut down?" Thoreau's *Journal* and books are full of precise observation of trees, especially pines — "Nothing stands up more free from blame in this world than a pine tree" – and lamentation at the demonic, as he termed it, leveling of forests in New England during his lifetime.

Thoreau on occasion astonished the people of Concord with his knowledge of trees, in particular his ability to date precisely the age of fallen or felled trees and to explain how trees propagate. Since then we have acquired much scientific insight into and data and theories about trees. Recent studies show that tree growth is correlated to levels of cosmic radiation arriving from distant stars. Probably this would not have surprised our ancestors who worshipped goddesses in groves of old-growth trees. It wouldn't surprise Gary Snyder, who writes of the pine, "Cybele's tree this, sacred in groves."

The majority of the poems in this book are less ecstatic than Homer and Dickey, less downcast than Hopkins and Thoreau, more formal or more familial or longer or wittier or downright more mysterious. And of course they are unscientific. Had I had more space, I could easily have added to the number of poems, but I am confident that all the poems here give pleasure in one way or another and invite rereading. We live among trees, and if we are to have a future we must be planters and keepers of trees.

Harry Thomas

In memory of Stanley Plumly, 1939–2019.

GLADNESS

From *THE ODYSSEY*

"Here I am at your mercy, princess –
are you a goddess or a mortal? If one of the gods
who rule the skies up there, you're Artemis to the life,
the daughter of mighty Zeus – I see her now – just
    look
at your build, your bearing, your lithe flowing
    grace ...
But if you're one of the mortals living here on earth,
three times blest are your father, your queenly mother,
three times over your brothers too. How often their
    hearts
must warm with joy to see you striding into the
    dances –
such a bloom of beauty. True, but he is the one
more blest than all other men alive, that man
who sways you with gifts and leads you home,
    his bride!
I have never laid eyes on anyone like you,
neither man nor woman ...
I look at you and a sense of wonder takes me.

                                  Wait,
once I saw the like – in Delos, beside Apollo's altar –
the young slip of a palm-tree springing into the light.
There I'd sailed, you see, with a great army in my
    wake,

out on the long campaign that doomed my life to
     hardship.
That vision! Just as I stood there gazing, rapt, for
     hours . . .
no shaft like that had ever risen up from the earth –
so now I marvel at *you*, my lady: rapt, enthralled,
too struck with awe to grasp you by the knees
though pain has ground me down."

NUTTING

                              —It seems a day
(I speak of one from many singled out)
One of those heavenly days that cannot die;
When, in the eagerness of boyish hope,
I left our cottage-threshold, sallying forth
With a huge wallet o'er my shoulders slung,
A nutting-crook in hand; and turned my steps
Tow'rd some far-distant wood, a Figure quaint,
Tricked out in proud disguise of cast-off weeds
Which for that service had been husbanded,
By exhortation of my frugal Dame –
Motley accoutrement, of power to smile
At thorns, and brakes, and brambles, – and in truth
More ragged than need was! O'er pathless rocks,
Through beds of matted fern, and tangled thickets,
Forcing my way, I came to one dear nook
Unvisited, where not a broken bough
Drooped with its withered leaves, ungracious sign
Of devastation; but the hazels rose
Tall and erect, with tempting clusters hung,
A virgin scene! – A little while I stood,
Breathing with such suppression of the heart
As joy delights in; and with wise restraint
Voluptuous, fearless of a rival, eyed
The banquet; – or beneath the trees I sate

Among the flowers, and with the flowers I played;
A temper known to those who, after long
And weary expectation, have been blest
With sudden happiness beyond all hope.
Perhaps it was a bower beneath whose leaves
The violets of five seasons re-appear
And fade, unseen by any human eye;
Where fairy water-breaks do murmur on
For ever; and I saw the sparkling foam,
And – with my cheek on one of those green stones
That, fleeced with moss, under the shady trees,
Lay round me, scattered like a flock of sheep –
I heard the murmur and the murmuring sound,
In that sweet mood when pleasure loves to pay
Tribute to ease; and, of its joy secure,
The heart luxuriates with indifferent things,
Wasting its kindliness on stocks and stones,
And on the vacant air. Then up I rose,
And dragged to earth both branch and bough,
          with crash
And merciless ravage: and the shady nook
Of hazels, and the green and mossy bower,
Deformed and sullied, patiently gave up
Their quiet being: and unless I now
Confound my present feelings with the past,
Ere from the mutilated bower I turned
Exulting, rich beyond the wealth of kings,

I felt a sense of pain when I beheld
The silent trees, and saw the intruding sky. –
Then, dearest Maiden, move along these shades
In gentleness of heart; with gentle hand
Touch – for there is a spirit in the woods.

THE ASH GROVE

Half of the grove stood dead, and those that yet lived
    made
Little more than the dead ones made of shade.
If they led to a home, long before they had seen its fall:
But they welcomed me; I was glad without cause
    and delayed.

Scarce a hundred paces under the trees was the
    interval –
Paces each sweeter than sweetest miles – but nothing
    at all,
Not even the spirits of memory and fear with restless
    wing,
Could climb down in to molest me over the wall

That I passed through at either end without noticing.
And now an ash grove far from those hills can bring
The same tranquillity in which I wander a ghost
With a ghostly gladness, as if I heard a girl sing

The song of the Ash Grove soft as love uncrossed,
And then in a crowd or in distance it were lost,
But the moment unveiled something unwilling to die
And I had what most I desired, without search or
    desert or cost.

ASH-BOUGHS

a.

Not of áll my eyes see, wandering on the world,
Is anything a milk to the mind so, so sighs deep
Poetry tó it, as a tree whose boughs break in the sky.
Say it is ásh-boughs: whether on a December day
     and furled
Fast ór they in clammyish lashtender combs creep
Apart wide and new-nestle at heaven most high.
They touch heaven, tabour on it; how their talons
     sweep
The smouldering enormous winter welkin! May
Mells blue and snow white through them, a fringe
     and fray
Of greenery: it is old earth's groping towards the steep
       Heaven whom she childs us by.

(Variant from line 7.)   *b.*

  They touch, they tabour on it, hover on it; here, there
      hurled,
        With talons sweep
  The smouldering enormous winter welkin. Eye,
        But more cheer is when May
  Mells blue with snowwhite through their fringe and fray
  Of greenery and old earth gropes for, grasps at steep
        Heaven with it whom she childs things by.

WOODS, A PROSE SONNET

Wise are ye, O ancient woods! wiser than man. Whoso goeth in your paths or into your thickets where no paths are, readeth the same cheerful lesson whether he be a young child or a hundred years old. Comes he in good fortune or bad, ye say the same things, & from age to age. Ever the needles of the pine grow & fall, the acorns on the oak, the maples redden in autumn, & at all times of the year the ground pine & the pyrola bud & root under foot. What is called fortune & what is called Time by men – ye know them not. Men have not language to describe one moment of your eternal life. This I would ask of you, o sacred Woods, when ye shall next give me somewhat to say, give me also the tune wherein to say it. Give me a tune of your own like your winds or rains or brooks or birds; for the songs of men grow old when they have been often repeated, but yours, though a man have heard them for seventy years, are never the same, but always new, like time itself, or like love.

A clump of white pines, seen far westward over the shrub oak plain, which is now lit up by the setting sun, a soft, feathery grove, with their gray stems indistinctly seen, like human beings come to their cabin door, standing expectant on the edge of the plain, impress me with a mild humanity. The trees indeed have hearts. With a certain affection the sun seems to send its farewell ray far and level over the copses to them, and they silently receive it with gratitude, like a group of settlers with their children. The pines impress me as human. A slight vaporous cloud floats high over them, while in the west the sun goes down apace behind glowing pines, and golden clouds like mountains skirt the horizon.

Nothing stands up more free from blame in this world than a pine tree.

ROOTS AND LEAVES THEMSELVES ALONE

Roots and leaves themselves alone are these,
Scents brought to men and women from the wild
    woods and pond-side,
Breast-sorrel and pinks of love, fingers that wind
    around tighter than vines,
Gushes from the throats of birds hid in the foliage of
    trees as the sun is risen,
Breezes of land and love set from living shores to you
    on the living sea, to you O sailors!
Frost-mellow'd berries and Third-month twigs offer'd
    fresh to young persons wandering out in the
    fields when the winter breaks up,
Love-buds put before you and within you whoever
    you are,
Buds to be unfolded on the old terms,
If you bring the warmth of the sun to them they will
    open and bring form, color, perfume, to you,
If you become the aliment and the wet they will
    become flowers, fruits, tall branches and trees.

TREES AND CATTLE

Many trees can stand unshaded
In this place where the sun is alone,
But some may break out.
They may be taken to Heaven,
So gold is my only sight.

Through me, two red cows walk;
From a crowning glory
Of slowness they are not taken.
Let one hoof knock on a stone,
And off it a spark jump quickly,

And fire may sweep these fields,
And all outburn the blind sun.
Like a new light I enter my life,
And hover, not yet consumed,
With the trees in holy alliance,

About to be offered up,
About to get wings where we stand.
The whole field stammers with gold;
No leaf but is actively still;
There is no quiet or noise;

Continually out of a fire
A bull walks forth,
And makes of my mind a red beast
At each step feeling how
The sun more deeply is burning

Because trees and cattle exist.
I go away, in the end.
In the shade, my bull's horns die
From my head; in some earthly way
I have been given my heart:

Behind my back, a tree leaps up
On wings that could save me from death.
Its branches dance over my head.
Its flight strikes a root in me.
A cow beneath it lies down.

LIGHTNING

It rained during the night.
The road has the smell of wet grass,
Then, again, the hand of the heat's
On our shoulder, as if
To say time will take nothing from us.

But there
Where the field comes up against the almond tree,
See, a fallow deer has leaped
From yesterday to today through the leaves.

And we stop, it isn't of this world.

And I come close to you,
I finish breaking you off from the blackened trunk,
Branch, summer-lightning struck,
From which yesterday's sap, heavenly still, runs.

YVES BONNEFOY (1923–2016)   35
TRANSLATED BY PASCALE TORRACINTA
AND HARRY THOMAS

TRAIN JOURNEY

Glassed with cold sleep and dazzled by the moon,
out of the confused hammering dark of the train
I looked and saw under the moon's cold sheet
your delicate dry breasts, country that built my heart;

and the small trees on their uncoloured slope
like poetry moved, articulate and sharp
and purposeful under the great dry flight of air,
under the crosswise currents of wind and star.

Clench down your strength, box-tree and ironbark.
Break with your violent root the virgin rock.
Draw from the flying dark its breath of dew
till the unliving come to life in you.

Be over the blind rock a skin of sense,
under the barren height a slender dance ...

I woke and saw the dark small trees that burn
suddenly into flowers more lovely than the white
     moon.

FLOWERING EUCALYPT IN AUTUMN

That slim creek out of the sky
the dried-blood western gum tree
is all stir in its high reaches:

its strung haze-blue foliage is dancing
points down in breezy mobs, swapping
pace and place in an all-over sway

retarded en masse by crimson blossom.
Bees still at work up there tack
around their exploded furry likeness

and the lawn underneath's a napped rug
of eyelash drift, of blooms flared
like a sneeze in a redhaired nostril,

minute urns, pinch-sized rockets
knocked down by winds, by night-creaking
fig-squirting bats, or the daily

parrot gang with green pocketknife wings.
Bristling food for tough delicate
raucous life, each flower comes

as a spray in its own turned vase,
a taut starburst, honeyed model
of the tree's fragrance crisping in your head.

When the Japanese plum tree
was shedding in spring, we speculated
there among the drizzling petals

what kind of exquisitely precious
artistic bloom might be gendered
in a pure ethereal compost

of petals potted as they fell.
From unpetalled gum-debris
we know what is grown continually,

a tower of fabulous swish tatters,
a map hoisted upright, a crusted
riverbed with up-country show towns.

WHITE OAKS ASCENDING

In the mind-weave,
at a thousand, ten
thousand feet, they all
lean in on one another,
snowy, hollow, still
gothic with winter.

And the few torn leaves
starved neutral back
into the spring before
this one, the one long since
gone black under the ice,
hold on, mark time –

they'll fall eventually,
once, twice, and
turn dark green again,
slowly, in detail.
And the few songbirds,
with their clear glass eyes

and heartbreaking voices,
stationed out of sight
in the high, cold crowns –
they'll sing true again,

and fly and fall to earth
awhile among the human.

And this is promised
too, that the wind left
trapped in the blue
alleys of the branches
will climb and clarify
in the still and risen air.

Let the stone gods
in their fountains
turn like clockwork –
they're no less rooted
in the rain, nor their marble
less perfection of the snow –

let the clay gods circle
in the fire. The body
piecemeal falls away;
the spirit, in the privacy
of dark, sheds all its leaves.
I died, I climbed a tree, I sang.

TOWARD AN ALPHABET OF TREES

LETTER FROM TOWN: THE ALMOND TREE

You promised to send me some violets. Did you forget?
  White ones and blue ones from under the orchard
    hedge?
  Sweet dark purple, and white ones mixed for
    a pledge
Of our early love that hardly has opened yet.

Here there's an almond tree – you have never seen
  Such a one in the north – it flowers on the street,
    and I stand
  Every day by the fence to look up at the flowers that
    expand
At rest in the blue, and wonder at what they mean.

Under the almond tree, the happy lands
  Provence, Japan, and Italy repose;
  And passing feet are chatter and clapping of those
Who play around us, country girls clapping their hands.

You, my love, the foremost, in a flowered gown,
  All your unbearable tenderness, you with the
    laughter
  Startled upon your eyes now so wide with hereafter,
You with loose hands of abandonment hanging down.

D. H. LAWRENCE (1885–1930)   43

THE APPLES

And what should one think
Of these yellow apples? Yesterday,
They surprised us, waiting that way, naked
After the fall of leaves.

Today they charm,
So modestly their shoulders
Are traced
By a scallop of snow.

ASPENS

All day and night, save winter, every weather,
Above the inn, the smithy, and the shop,
The aspens at the cross-roads talk together
Of rain, until their last leaves fall from the top.

Out of the blacksmith's cavern comes the ringing
Of hammer, shoe, and anvil; out of the inn
The clink, the hum, the roar, the random singing –
The sounds that for these fifty years have been.

The whisper of the aspens is not drowned,
And over lightless pane and footless road,
Empty as sky, with every other sound
Not ceasing, calls their ghosts from their abode,

A silent smithy, a silent inn, nor fails
In the bare moonlight or the thick-furred gloom,
In tempest or the night of nightingales,
To turn the cross-roads to a ghostly room.

And it would be the same were no house near.
Over all sorts of weather, men, and times,
Aspens must shake their leaves and men may hear
But need not listen, more than to my rhymes.

Whatever wind blows, while they and I have leaves
We cannot other than an aspen be
That ceaselessly, unreasonably grieves,
Or so men think who like a different tree.

LOVELIEST OF TREES

Loveliest of trees, the cherry now
Is hung with bloom along the bough,
And stands about the woodland ride
Wearing white for Eastertide.

Now, of my threescore years and ten,
Twenty will not come again,
And take from seventy springs a score,
It only leaves me fifty more.

And since to look at things in bloom
Fifty springs are little room,
About the woodlands I will go
To see the cherry hung with snow.

"FROM ALL THESE TREES"

From all these trees,
in the salads, the soup, everywhere,
cherry blossoms fall.

THE HORSE CHESTNUT TREE

Boys in sporadic but tenacious droves
Come with sticks, as certainly as Autumn,
To assault the great horse chestnut tree.

There is a law governs their lawlessness.
Desire is in them for a shining amulet
And the best are those that are highest up.

They will not pick them easily from the ground.
With shrill arms they fling to the higher branches,
To hurry the work of nature for their pleasure.

I have seen them trooping down the street
Their pockets stuffed with chestnuts shucked,
        unshucked.
It is only evening keeps them from their wish.

Sometimes I run out in a kind of rage
To chase the boys away: I catch an arm,
Maybe, and laugh to think of being the lawgiver.

I was once such a young sprout myself
And fingered in my pocket the prize and trophy.
But still I moralize upon the day

And see that we, outlaws on God's property,
Fling out imagination beyond the skies,
Wishing a tangible good from the unknown.

And likewise death will drive us from the scene
With the great flowering world unbroken yet,
Which we held in idea, a little handful.

COCO-DE-MER

It's rumoured that on the island
there's a particular tree
that drops these enormous coconuts
known as "coco-de-mer" in the sea.

Some of these trees are male
and some female: they live
quite apart from each other
in their separate coconut-groves.

On one night in the year, however,
they shake the mud off their roots and veer
towards each other
for a bit of how's-your-father.

Limb upon flailing limb:
branches and roots enmeshed;
anyone who witnesses this tree-tryst
will at once turn into a heap of mush

or a pillar of salt. I myself and my companion
were coming home late at night: we heard such
a commotion behind us
that we immediately faced into the ditch

and didn't dare look back
or light a match or move a muscle
as the trees went jumbering past
with their judders and jolts and jostles.

TO A DRIED-UP ELM

After the rains of April and the suns of May,
the old, blasted elm,
half eaten away,
has just put forth a few green leaves.

The century-old elm up on the hill
past which the Duero flows! Dull
yellow moss badges the whitened bark
on its dusty, carious trunk.

Unlike the song-filled poplars
lining the road and the riverbank,
it won't be the home of nightingales.

Dauntless ants in single file
make their ascent, and in its entrails
spiders drape their drab, grey webs.

Before you fall, elm of the Duero,
to the woodman's axe and the carpenter
planes you down for a church bell's brace,
a carriage axle or the yoke of a cart;
before you redden, tomorrow, in the grate
of some forlorn abode
huddled beside the country road;

before you're torn up by a dust devil
or felled by a gust from the white sierras;
before the river takes you, elm, to the sea
hurtling through valleys and ravines,
I want to preserve, here in my notebook,
the sudden grace of your green-clad branch.
Turned to the light, to the life it might bring,
my heart as much as yours awaits
another miracle of Spring.

54 ANTONIO MACHADO (1875–1939)
TRANSLATED BY JAMIE McKENDRICK

EUCALYPTS IN EXILE

They've had so many jobs:
boiling African porridge. Being printed on.
Sopping up malaria. Flying in Paris uprisings.
Supporting a stork's nest in Spain.

Their suits are neater abroad,
of denser drape, un-nibbled:
they've left their parasites at home.

They flower out of bullets
and, without any taproot,
draw water from way deep.
Blown down in high winds
they reveal the black sun of that trick.

Standing around among shed limbs
and loose craquelure of bark
is home-country stuff
but fire is ingrained.
They explode the mansions of Malibu
because to be eucalypts
they have to shower sometimes in Hell.

Their humans, meeting them abroad,
often grab and sniff their hands.

Loveable singly or unmarshalled
they are merciless in a gang.

THE FIG TREE

When it grew hot and figs were filled with milk,
Your doves appeared and tore the purple skin.
Their black eyes ringed in white, with throats of silk,
They pillaged bird-limed boughs, unseen within
Your leaves. They took what I with caution pick:
This not quite seemly fig, this gem of lust,
Confused with knowledge, making seasons sick
With songs of fevered morals we kept hushed.
But she with slackened branches waits here now.
And losing leaves won't lessen my regard,
She is immovable as peach or pear;
But once before, as now, He asked her how
She had no fruit for those who labored hard,
And cursed and curled with hate her leafy hair.

GINKGOES IN FALL

They are the oldest living captive race,
Primitive gymnosperms that in the wild
Are rarely found or never, temple trees
Brought down in line unbroken from the deep
Past where the Yellow Emperor lies tombed.

Their fallen yellow fruit mimics the scent
Of human vomit, the definite statement of
An attitude, and their translucency of leaf,
Filtering a urinary yellow light,
Remarks a delicate wasting of the world,

An innuendo to be clarified
In winter when they defecate their leaves
And bear the burden of their branches up
Alone and bare, dynastic diagrams
Of their distinguished genealogies.

THE LEMON TREES

Hear me a moment. Laureate poets
seem to wander among plants
no one knows: boxwood, acanthus,
where nothing is alive to touch.
I prefer small streets that falter
into grassy ditches where a boy,
searching in the sinking puddles,
might capture a struggling eel.
The little path that winds down
along the slope plunges through cane-tufts
and opens suddenly into the orchard
among the moss-green trunks
of the lemon trees.

Perhaps it is better
if the jubilee of small birds
dies away, swallowed in the sky,
yet more real to one who listens,
the murmur of leaves
in a breathless, moving air.
The senses are filled with an odor
filled with the earth.
It is like rain in a troubled breast,
sweet as an air can that arrives
too suddenly and vanishes.

A miracle is hushed; all passions
are swept aside. Even the poor
know that richness,
the fragrance of the lemon trees.

You realize that in silences
things yield and almost betray
their ultimate secrets.
At times, one half expects
to discover an error in Nature,
the still point of reality,
the missing link that will not hold,
the thread we cannot untangle
in order to get at the truth.
You look around. Your mind seeks,
makes harmonies, falls apart
in the perfume, expands
when the day wearies away.
There are silences in which one watches
in every fading human shadow
something divine let go.

The illusion dies, and in time we return
to our noisy cities where the blue
appears only in fragments
high up among the towering shapes.
Then rain leaching the earth.

Tedious, winter burdens the roofs,
and light is a miser, the soul bitter.
Yet, one day through an open gate,
among the green luxuriance of a yard,
the yellow lemons fire
and the heart melts,
and the golden songs pour
into the breast
from the raised cornets of the sun.

EUGENIO MONTALE (1896–1981)

TRANSLATED BY LEE GERLACH

THE MAPLE TREE

The Maple with its tassell flowers of green
That turns to red a stag horn shaped seed
Just spreading out its scallopped leaves is seen
Of yellowish hue yet beautifully green
Bark ribb'd like corderoy in seamy screed
That farther up the stem is smoother seen
Where the white hemlock with white umbel flowers
Up each spread stoven to the branches towers
And mossy round the stoven spread dark green
And blotched leaved orchis and the blue bell flowers
Thickly they grow and neath the leaves are seen
I love to see them gemm'd with morning hours
I love the lone green places where they be
And the sweet clothing of the Maple tree

I SAW IN LOUISIANA A LIVE-OAK GROWING

I saw in Louisiana a live-oak growing,
All alone stood it and the moss hung down from the
    branches,
Without any companion it grew there uttering joyous
    leaves of dark green,
And its look, rude, unbending, lusty, made me think of
    myself,
But I wonder'd how it could utter joyous leaves
    standing alone there without its friend near, for
    I knew I could not,
And I broke off a twig with a certain number of leaves
    upon it, and twined around it a little moss,
And brought it away, and I have placed it in sight in
    my room,
It is not needed to remind me as of my own dear
    friends,
(For I believe lately I think of little else than of them,)
Yet it remains to me a curious token, it makes me
    think of manly love;
For all that, and though the live-oak glistens there in
    Louisiana solitary in a wide flat space,
Uttering joyous leaves all its life without a friend
    a lover near,
I know very well I could not.

WALT WHITMAN (1819–92)

TO THE OAK

If I love you
I won't imitate the morning glory
Borrowing your high branches to display myself;
If I love you
I won't imitate those infatuated birds
Who repeat their monotonous flattery to the foliage,
Nor the fountain
With its solace of cool waters;
I won't even be those background vistas
That serve to make you more majestic.
Not even sunshine,
Not even spring rain,
No, none of these!
I would like to be a kapok tree
Standing beside you as an equal,
Our roots touching underground,
Our leaves touching in the clouds;
And with every gust of wind
We would bow to each other.
But no one else
Understands our language;
You have your branches
Like daggers or swords
While my big red flowers
Are heavy sighs.

Though it seems we are separated forever
We are eternally together.
This is great love,
This is fidelity.
Love –
Not only for your splendid trunk
But also for the earth you stand on.

SHU TING (1952–)

TRANSLATED BY CAROLYN KIZER

THE OLIVE TREE

In your hollow, nests a swarm of bees,
Old olive tree – you who are bowed beneath
A little green as yet, scant olive wreath –
As if they would intone your obsequies.

And every little bird, tipsy with love,
Chirruping among the boughs above,
Begins to give chase in their amorous bower,
Your branches that will no more come in flower.

How, at your dying, they will fill your arms
With their enchanting noise, and all the charms,
The liveliness, the loveliness, of youth,

Crowding your heart like memories. In truth,
I wish that souls could perish as you do –
The souls that are the sister souls to you.

TRANSLATED BY A. E. STALLINGS

THE ROYAL PALMS OF SOUTH FLORIDA

They line the streets like stoic palace guards
Stripped of all their pomp, or a colonnade
Of big-haired caryatids with nothing but porches

Of sky to support. Entasis gentles each trunk
Like a slight paunch, and fronds float in the air
As a catch of catfish, strung to a dock

And forgotten, might float, ghostly and skeletal,
After a few days in the Intracoastal.
They look like local South Americas

To renegade parakeets, and their gray trunks
Are endless lizard skyways, paved with dirty,
Lichened cement. They could be flagstaffs flying

Wind-shredded flags, or extras in a movie
About exiled rulers in a dull new world.

THE PURPLE PEACH TREE

Timidly, still half asleep, it has blossomed.
Afraid of the teeth of the frost, it was late this year.
Now its crimson mixes with the
Brilliance of the cherries and apricots.
Unique, it is more beautiful than snow and hoar frost.
Under the cold, its heart awoke to the Spring season.
Full of wine, sprawling on the alabaster table,
I dream of the ancient poet who could not distinguish
The peach, the cherry and the apricot, except by their
Green leaves and dark branches.

TRANSLATED BY KENNETH REXROTH

PEAR TREE

Silver dust,
lifted from the earth,
higher than my arms reach,
you have mounted,
O, silver,
higher than my arms reach,
you front us with great mass;

no flower ever opened
so staunch a white leaf,
no flower ever parted silver
from such rare silver;

O, white pear,
your flower-tufts
thick on the branch
bring summer and ripe fruits
in their purple hearts.

H. D. (1886–1961)

LIMBER PINES

Limber pines are the suicide trees, nothing holding
    back their
sensibilities, and nothing to make them say what it is
    they feel as
they rush into clearings like people fleeing a movie
    house in flames
or jumping from a sundered ship into a burning sea.
                                 Their weakness
is their ability to take hold anywhere.
                               Their strength is their ability
to die.
   They are the bark beetle's favorite lunch, the
    wildfire's
favorite witch, the wind's best game of dominoes.
                               Sometimes you
see one clinging to a sunwashed rock, like the
    castaway a little later,
but limber pines can squeeze blood from a stone and
    drink it.
                                      Their
roots crack granite, hold, live on next to nothing and,
    stunted, grow
into wizened children.

THE PLUM-TREE

The back-yard has a tiny plum-tree,
It shows how small a tree can be.
Yet there it is, railed round
So no one tramps it to the ground.

It's reached its full shape, low and meagre.
O yes, it wants to grow more, it's eager
For what can't be done –
It gets too little sun.

A plum-tree no hand's ever been at
To pick a plum: it strains belief.
It is a plum-tree for all that –
We know it by the leaf.

BERTOLT BRECHT (1896–1956)   71
TRANSLATED BY EDWIN MORGAN

THE MAD POMEGRANATE TREE

Inquisitive matinal high spirits à perdre haleine

In these all-white courtyards where the south wind
    blows
Whistling through vaulted arcades, tell me, is it the
    mad pomegranate tree
That leaps in the light, scattering its fruitful laughter
With windy wilfulness and whispering, tell me, is it
    the mad pomegranate tree
That quivers with foliage newly born at dawn
Raising high its colors in a shiver of triumph?

On plains where the naked girls awake,
When they harvest clover with their light brown arms
Roaming round the borders of their dreams – tell me,
    is it the mad pomegranate tree,
Unsuspecting, that puts the lights in their verdant
    baskets
That floods their names with the singing of birds –
    tell me
Is it the mad pomegranate tree that combats the
    cloudy skies of the world?

On the day that it adorns itself in jealousy with seven
     kinds of feathers,
Girding the eternal sun with a thousand blinding
     prisms
Tell me, is it the mad pomegranate tree
That seizes on the run a horse's mane of a hundred
     lashes,
Never sad and never grumbling – tell me, is it the mad
     pomegranate tree
That cries out the new hope now dawning?

Tell me, is that the mad pomegranate tree waving in
     the distance,
Fluttering a handkerchief of leaves of cool flame,
A sea near birth with a thousand ships and more,
With waves that a thousand times and more set out
     and go
To unscented shores – tell me, is it the mad
     pomegranate tree
That creaks the rigging aloft in the lucid air?

High as can be, with the blue bunch of grapes that
     flares and celebrates
Arrogant, full of danger – tell me, is it the mad
     pomegranate tree

73

That shatters with light the demon's tempests in the
    middle of the world
That spreads far as can be the saffron ruffle of day
Richly embroidered with scattered songs – tell me, is
    it the mad pomegranate tree
That hastily unfastens the silk apparel of day?

In petticoats of April first and cicadas of the feast of
    mid-August
Tell me, that which plays, that which rages, that which
    can entice
Shaking out of threats their evil black darkness
Spilling in the sun's embrace intoxicating birds
Tell me, that which opens its wings on the breast of
    things
On the breast of our deepest dreams, is that the mad
    pomegranate tree?

    TRANSLATED BY EDMUND KEELEY
    AND PHILLIP SHERRARD

THE REDWOODS

Mountains are moving, rivers
are hurrying. But we
are still.

We have the thoughts of giants –
clouds, and at night the stars.

And we have names – guttural, grotesque –
Hamet, Og – names with no syllables.

And perish, one by one, our roots
gnawed by the mice. And fall.

And are too slow for death, and change
to stone. Or else too quick,

like candles in a fire. Giants
are lonely. We have waited long

for someone. By our waiting, surely
there must be someone at whose touch

our boughs would bend; and hands
to gather us; a spirit

to whom we are light as the hawthorn tree.
O if there is a poet

let him come now! We stand at the Pacific
like great unmarried girls,

turning in our heads the stars and clouds,
considering whom to please.

YOUNG SYCAMORE

I must tell you
this young tree
whose round and firm trunk
between the wet

pavement and the gutter
(where water
is trickling) rises
bodily

into the air with
one undulant
thrust half its height –
and then

dividing and waning
sending out
young branches on
all sides –

hung with cocoons
it thins
till nothing is left of it
but two

eccentric knotted
twigs
bending forward
hornlike at the top

THE TULIP TREE

Many a winter night
the green of the tulip tree
lives again among other trees,
returns through miles of rain
to that level of color
all day pattered, wind-wearied,
calmly asserted in our yard.

Only pale by the evergreen,
hardly distinguished by leaf or color,
it used to slide a little pale from other trees
and – no great effect at our house –
it sustained what really belonged
but would, if severely doubted,
disappear.

Many a winter night
it arrives and says for a moment:
"I am still here."

WILLIAM STAFFORD (1914–93)   79

THE WILLOWS OF MASSACHUSETTS

Animal willows of November
in pelt of gold enduring when all else
has let go all ornament
and stands naked in the cold.
Cold shine of sun on swamp water,
cold caress of slant beam on bough,
gray light on brown bark.
Willows – last to relinquish a leaf,
curious, patient, lion-headed, tense
with energy, watching
the serene cold through a curtain
of tarnished strands.

YEW-TREES

There is a Yew-tree, pride of Lorton Vale,
Which to this day stands single, in the midst
Of its own darkness, as it stood of yore;
Not loth to furnish weapons for the bands
Of Umfraville or Percy ere they marched
To Scotland's heaths; or those that crossed the sea
And drew their sounding bows at Azincour,
Perhaps at earlier Crecy, or Poictiers.
Of vast circumference and gloom profound
This solitary Tree! a living thing
Produced too slowly ever to decay;
Of form and aspect too magnificent
To be destroyed. But worthier still of note
Are those fraternal Four of Borrowdale,
Joined in one solemn and capacious grove;
Huge trunks! and each particular trunk a growth
Of intertwisted fibres serpentine
Up-coiling, and inveterately convolved;
Nor uninformed with Phantasy, and looks
That threaten the profane; – a pillared shade,
Upon whose grassless floor of red-brown hue,
By sheddings from the pining umbrage tinged
Perennially – beneath whose sable roof
Of boughs, as if for festal purpose, decked
With unrejoicing berries – ghostly Shapes

May meet at noontide; Fear and trembling Hope,
Silence and Foresight; Death the Skeleton
And Time the Shadow; – there to celebrate,
As in a natural temple scattered o'er
With altars undisturbed of mossy stone,
United worship; or in mute repose
To lie, and listen to the mountain flood
Murmuring from Glaramara's inmost caves.

PLANTING AND PRESERVING

From *THE GEORGICS*

The trees that rise up of their own free will
Into the light, wild, happy in the strength
They got from nature's power in the earth,
Do not bear fruit of their own spontaneous selves;
But if they're grafted, or taken up and replanted,
In holes that have been carefully prepared,
They'll give up their wildness, and, with frequent
      tilling,
Be ready to learn whatever you want them to learn.
It's just that way if you cut a barren stem
From low down on a tree and transplant it out
In an open sunlit field; left as it was,
It would be overshadowed by the abundant
Leaves and branches of its mother tree,
And its blighted berries would shrivel and dry up,
Even as they tried to grow. And the tree that arises
From seeds that fell and scattered on the ground
Develops slowly and lives to give its shade
To many later generations; its fruit
Is degenerate, having long ago forgotten
Its ancient taste, and it hangs in unsightly clusters,
Fit for nothing but for birds to ransack.

In every case hard work goes into the task
Of ordering the trees, a lot of work

To bring them under control. Stakes are the best
Supports for olives, and layering's best for vines,
Myrtles do best when the solid stem is planted;
You can propagate the hazel, whose wood is so hard,
From little slips; also the poplar tree,
Whose leaves Hercules plucked to make his crown;
So too the great Chaonian oak; the towering
Palm tree grows from slips; and the silver fir
That's born to know the dangers of the seas.
With a walnut shoot; and the sterile plane has often
Been seen to carry vigorous apple boughs;
White chestnut flowers have blossomed on the beech;
Pear-tree flowers have blossomed on the ash;
And swine have fed on acorns under the elm.

Stock-grafting and bud-grafting aren't the same:
In the place on a tree where the buds are just
    emerging
And breaking through their tender sheaths, a thin
Incision is cut, just at that place, and then
A bud from another tree is introduced
Into that slit, where the bark is full of sap,
And it's taught to grow and develop where it is.
In the instance of stock-grafting the cut is made
Where knots are absent, and therefore wedges
    are used
To open a path deep into the solid wood,

And then a slip from some fruitful other tree
Is introduced, and it isn't long before
A new great tree is towering toward the sky,
Exulting in its boughs, and full of wonder
At its foliage and its fruit, so unfamiliar.

VIRGIL (70–19BC)
TRANSLATED BY DAVID FERRY

THE PINE PLANTERS
(*Marty South's Reverie*)

I

We work here together
  In blast and breeze;
He fills the earth in,
  I hold the trees.

He does not notice
  That what I do
Keeps me from moving
  And chills me through.

He has seen one fairer
  I feel by his eye,
Which skims me as though
  I were not by.

And since she passed here
  He scarce has known
But that the woodland
  Holds him alone.

I have worked here with him
  Since morning shine,
He busy with his thoughts
  And I with mine.

I have helped him so many,
　　So many days,
But never win any
　　Small word of praise!

Shall I not sigh to him
　　That I work on
Glad to be nigh to him
　　Though hope is gone?

Nay, though he never
　　Knew love like mine,
I'll bear it ever
　　And make no sign!

II

From the bundle at hand here
　　I take each tree,
And set it to stand, here
　　Always to be;
When, in a second,
　　As if from fear
Of Life unreckoned
　　Beginning here,
It starts a sighing
　　Through day and night,
Though while there lying
　　'Twas voiceless quite.

It will sigh in the morning,
　　Will sigh at noon,
At the winter's warning,
　　In wafts of June;
Grieving that never
　　Kind Fate decreed
It should for ever
　　Remain a seed,
And shun the welter
　　Of things without,
Unneeding shelter
　　From storm and drought.

Thus, all unknowing
　　For whom or what
We set it growing
　　In this bleak spot,
It still will grieve here
　　Throughout its time,
Unable to leave here,
　　Or change its clime;
Or tell the story
　　Of us to-day
When, halt and hoary,
　　We pass away.

THE RACIAL LAWS

The magnolia right in the middle
of our Ferrara house's garden is the very
same that reappears in almost every
book of mine

We planted it in '39
ceremoniously
just a few months after
the Racial Laws were brought to bear
it was a solemn-comical affair all of us
fairly light-hearted God permitting despite
that irksome immemorial appendix
Judaism

Walled-in by four walls forewarned
soon enough it grew
black luminous intrusive
pointing firmly up towards the imminent
sky
full day
and night with grey
sparrows dusky blackbirds
unflaggingly scanned from below by pregnant
cats and by my
mother –

she too in tireless vigil there behind
the windowsill forever brimming
with her crumbs,

Straight as a sword from its base to its tip
now it overtops the neighboring roofs
beholding every bit of the city and the infinite
green space that circles it
but now somehow stumped I can guess
how it feels frail-tipped unsure
of a stretch up there in the heights a narrow space
in the sun
like someone at a loss
after a long journey
as to which road to take or
what to do

THE CAMPERDOWN ELM
Gift of Mr. A. G. Burgess to Prospect Park,
Brooklyn, 1872.

I think, in connection with this weeping elm,
of "Kindred Spirits" at the edge of a rockledge
    overlooking a stream:
Thanatopsis-invoking tree-loving Bryant
conversing with Timothy Cole
in Asher Durand's painting of them
under the filigree of an elm overhead.

No doubt they had seen other trees – lindens,
maples and sycamores, oaks and the Paris
street-tree, the horse-chestnut; but imagine
their rapture, had they come on the Camperdown elm's
massiveness and "the intricate pattern of its branches,"
arching high, curving low, in its mist of fine twigs.
The Bartlett tree-cavity specialist saw it
and thrust his arm the whole length of the hollowness
of its torso and there were six small cavities also.

Props are needed and tree-food. It is still leafing;
still there; *mortal* though. We must save it. It is
    our crowning curio.

MARIANNE MOORE (1887–1972)

THE BLACK WALNUT TREE

My mother and I debate:
we could sell
the black walnut tree
to the lumberman,
and pay off the mortgage.
Likely some storm anyway
will churn down its dark boughs,
smashing the house. We talk
slowly, two women trying
in a difficult time to be wise.
Roots in the cellar drains,
I say, and she replies
that the leaves are getting heavier
every year, and the fruit
harder to gather away.
But something brighter than money
moves in our blood – an edge
sharp and quick as a trowel
that wants us to dig and sow.
So we talk, but we don't do
anything. That night I dream
of my fathers out of Bohemia
filling the blue fields
of fresh and generous Ohio
with leaves and vines and orchards.

What my mother and I both know
is that we'd crawl with shame
in the emptiness we'd made
in our own and our fathers' backyard.
So the black walnut tree
swings through another year
of sun and leaping winds,
of leaves and bounding fruit,
and, month after month, the whip-
crack of the mortgage.

LANDSCAPE, DENSE WITH TREES

When you move away, you see how much depends
on the pace of the days – how much
depended on the haze we waded through
each summer, visible heat, wavy and discursive
as the lazy track of the snake in the dusty road;
and on the habit in town of porches thatched in vines,
and in the country long dense promenades, the way
we sacrificed the yards to shade.
It was partly the heat that made my father
plant so many trees – two maples marking the site
for the house, two elms on either side when it was
       done;
mimosa by the fence, and as it failed, fast-growing
       chestnuts,
loblolly pines; and dogwood, redbud, ornamental crab.
On the farm, everything else he grew
something could eat, but this
would be a permanent mark of his industry,
a glade established in the open field. Or so it seemed.
Looking back at the empty house from across the hill,
I see how well the house is camouflaged, see how
that porous fence of saplings, their later
scrim of foliage, thickened around it,
and still he chinked and mortared, planting more.
Last summer, although he'd lost all tolerance for heat,

he backed the truck in at the family grave
and stood in the truckbed all afternoon, pruning
the landmark oak, repairing recent damage by a wind;
then he came home and hung a swing
in one of the horse-chestnuts for my visit.
The heat was a hand at his throat,
a fist to his weak heart. But it made a triumph
of the cooler air inside, in the bedroom,
in the maple bedstead where he slept,
in the brick house nearly swamped by leaves.

BEECH TREE

I planted in February
A bronze-leafed beech,
In the chill brown soil
I spread out its silken fibres.

Protected it from the goats
With wire netting
And fixed it firm against
The worrying wind.

Now it is safe, I said,
April must stir
My precious baby
To greenful loveliness.

It is August now, I have hoped
But I hope no more –
My beech tree will never hide sparrows
From hungry hawks.

PLANTING THE ALDER

For the bark, dulled argent, roundly wrapped
And pigeon-collared.

For the splitter-splatter, guttering
Rain-flirt leaves.

For the snub and clot of the first green cones,
Smelted emerald, chlorophyll.

For the scut and scat of cones in winter,
So rattle-skinned, so fossil-brittle.

For the alder-wood, flame-red when torn
Branch from branch.

But mostly for the swinging locks
Of yellow catkins,

Plant it, plant it,
Streel-head in the rain.

SEAMUS HEANEY (1939–2013)

PLANTING A SEQUOIA

All afternoon my brothers and I have worked in the
　　　orchard,
Digging this hole, laying you into it, carefully packing
　　　the soil.
Rain blackened the horizon, but cold winds kept it
　　　over the Pacific,
And the sky above us stayed the dull gray
Of an old year coming to an end.

In Sicily a father plants a tree to celebrate his first
　　　son's birth –
An olive or a fig tree – a sign that the earth has one
　　　more life to bear.
I would have done the same, proudly laying new stock
　　　into my father's orchard,
A green sapling rising among the twisted apple boughs,
A promise of new fruit in other autumns.

But today we kneel in the cold planting you, our native
　　　giant,
Defying the practical custom of our fathers,
Wrapping in your roots a lock of hair, a piece of an
　　　infant's birth cord,
All that remains above earth of a first-born son,
A few stray atoms brought back to the elements.

We will give you what we can – our labor and our soil,
Water drawn from the earth when the skies fail,
Nights scented with the ocean fog, days softened by
    the circuit of bees.
We plant you in the corner of the grove, bathed in
    western light,
A slender shoot against the sunset.

And when our family is no more, all of his unborn
    brothers dead,
Every niece and nephew scattered, the house torn
    down,
His mother's beauty ashes in the air,
I want you to stand among strangers, all young and
    ephemeral to you,
Silently keeping the secret of your birth.

From *THE MAN WHO PLANTED TREES*

The shepherd went to fetch a small sack and poured out a heap of acorns on the table. He began to inspect them, one by one, with great concentration, separating the good from the bad. I smoked my pipe. I did offer to help him. He told me that it was his job. And in fact, seeing the care he devoted to the task, I did not insist. That was the whole of our conversation. When he had set aside a large enough pile of good acorns he counted them out by tens, meanwhile eliminating the small ones or those which were slightly cracked, for now he examined them more closely. When he had thus selected one hundred perfect acorns he stopped and we went to bed.

There was peace in being with this man. The next day I asked if I might rest here for a day. He found it quite natural – or, to be more exact, he gave me the impression that nothing could startle him. The rest was not absolutely necessary, but I was interested and wished to know more about him. He opened the pen and led his flock to pasture. Before leaving, he plunged his sack of carefully selected and counted acorns into a pail of water.

I noticed that he carried for a stick an iron rod as thick as my thumb and about a yard and a half long. Resting myself by walking, I followed a path parallel to his. His pasture was in a valley. He left the dog in charge of the little flock and climbed toward where I stood. I was afraid that he was about to rebuke me for my indiscretion, but it was not that at all: this was the way he was going, and he invited me to go along if I had nothing better to do. He climbed to the top of the ridge, about a hundred yards away.

There he began thrusting his iron rod into the earth, making a hole in which he planted an acorn; then he refilled the hole. He was planting oak trees. I asked him if the land belonged to him. He answered no. Did he know whose it was? He did not. He supposed it was community property, or perhaps belonged to people who cared nothing about it. He was not interested in finding out whose it was. He planted his hundred acorns with the greatest care.

After the midday meal he resumed his planting. I suppose I must have been fairly insistent in my questioning, for he answered me. For three years he had been planting trees in this wilderness. He had planted one hundred thousand. Of the hundred thousand, twenty thousand had sprouted. Of the twenty thousand he still expected to lose about half, to rodents or to the unpredictable designs of Providence. There remained ten thousand oak trees to grow where nothing had grown before.

PLACE

On the last day of the world
I would want to plant a tree

what for
not for the fruit

the tree that bears the fruit
is not the one that was planted

I want the tree that stands
in the earth for the first time

with the sun already
going down

and the water
touching its roots

in the earth full of the dead
and the clouds passing

one by one
over its leaves

104 W. S. MERWIN (1927–2019)

GROVE, WOODS,
ORCHARD, FOREST

From *THE ODYSSEY*

At that she touched the mules with her shining whip
and they quickly left the running stream behind.
The team trotted on, their hoofs wove in and out.
She drove them back with care so all the rest,
maids and Odysseus, could keep the pace on foot,
and she used the whip discreetly.
The sun sank as they reached the hallowed grove,
sacred to Athena, where Odysseus stopped and sat
and said a prayer at once to mighty Zeus's daughter:
"Hear me, daughter of Zeus whose shield is thunder –
tireless one, Athena! Now hear my prayer at last,
for you never heard me then, when I was shattered,
when the famous god of earthquakes wrecked my
    craft.
Grant that here among the Phaeacian people
I may find some mercy and some love!"

HOMER (8TH CENTURY BC)   107
TRANSLATED BY ROBERT FAGLES

THE BIRCH GROVE

At the back of a garden, in earshot of river water,
In a corner walled off like the baths or bake-house
Of an unroofed abbey or broken-floored Roman villa,
They have planted their birch grove. Planted it
    recently only,
But already each morning it puts forth in the sun
Like their own long grown-up selves, the white of
    the bark
As suffused and cool as the white of the satin
    nightdress
She bends and straightens up in, pouring tea,
Sitting across from where he dandles a sandal
On his big time-keeping foot, as bare as an abbot's.
Red brick and slate, plum tree and apple retain
Their credibility, a CD of Bach is making the rounds
Of the common or garden air. Above them a jet trail
Tapers and waves like a willow wand or a taper.
"If art teaches us anything," he says, trumping life
With a quote, "it's that the human condition is
    private."

"NOT A LEAF STIRRING"

Not a leaf stirring;
frightening,
    the summer grove.

YOSA BUSON (1716–83)

TRANSLATED BY ROBERT HASS

A SMALL GROVE IN TORRI DEL BENACO

Outside our window we have a small willow, and a little beyond it a fig tree, and then a stone shed. Beyond the stone the separate trees suddenly become a grove: a lemon, a mimosa, an oleander, a pine, one of the tall slender cypresses that a poet here once called candles of darkness that ought to be put out in winter, another willow, and a pine.

She stands among them in her flowered green clothes. Her skin is darker gold than the olives in the morning sun. Two hours ago we got up and bathed in the lake. It was like swimming in a vein. Everything that can blossom is blossoming around her now. She is the eye of the grove, the eye of mimosa and willow. The cypress behind her catches fire.

NOT DEAD

Walking through trees to cool my heat and pain,
I know that David's with me here again.
All that is simple, happy, strong, he is.
Caressingly I stroke
Rough bark of the friendly oak.
A brook goes bubbling by: the voice is his.
Turf burns with pleasant smoke;
I laugh at chaffinch and at primroses.
All that is simple, happy, strong, he is.
Over the whole wood in a little while
Breaks his slow smile.

THE FRIENDLY WOOD

We were thinking of things pure,
side by side, along the paths,
we were holding hands
without speaking ... among the dark flowers.

We strolled like a couple betrothed,
alone, in the green night of the fields,
sharing the fruit of fairyland
the moon friendly to madness.

And then we lay dead on the moss,
far away, all alone, in the soft shadows
of the intimate murmuring wood;

And above us, in the immense light,
we found ourselves weeping
oh my dear companion of silence!

112 PAUL VALÉRY (1871–1945)
TRANSLATED BY C. F. MacINTYRE
AND J. LAUGHLIN

WOODS
(*For Nicolas Nabokov*)

Sylvan meant savage in those primal woods
Piero di Cosimo so loved to draw,
Where nudes, bears, lions, sows with women's heads,
Mounted and murdered and ate each other raw,
Nor thought the lightning-kindled bush to tame
But, flabbergasted, fled the useful flame.

Reduced to patches, owned by hunting squires,
Of villages with ovens and a stocks,
They whispered still of most unsocial fires,
Though Crown and Mitre warned their silly flocks
The pasture's humdrum rhythms to approve
And to abhor the licence of the grove.

Guilty intention still looks for a hotel
That wants no details and surrenders none;
A wood is that, and throws in charm as well,
And many a semi-innocent, undone,
Has blamed its nightingales who round the deed
Sang with such sweetness of a happy greed.

Those birds, of course, did nothing of the sort,
And, as for sylvan nature, if you take
A snapshot at a picnic, O how short
And lower-ordersy the Gang will look
By those vast lives that never took another
And are not scared of gods, ghosts, or stepmother.

Among these coffins of its by-and-by
The Public can (it cannot on a coast)
Bridle its skirt-and-bargain-chasing eye,
And where should an austere philologist
Relax but in the very world of shade
From which the matter of his field was made.

Old sounds re-educate an ear grown coarse,
As Pan's green father suddenly raps out
A burst of undecipherable Morse,
And cuckoos mock in Welsh, and doves create
In rustic English over all they do
To rear their modern family of two.

Now here, now there, some loosened element,
A fruit in vigour or a dying leaf,
Utters its private idiom for descent,
And late man, listening through his latter grief,
Hears, close or far, the oldest of his joys,
Exactly as it was, the water noise.

A well-kempt forest begs Our Lady's grace;
Someone is not disgusted, or at least
Is laying bets upon the human race
Retaining enough decency to last;
The trees encountered on a country stroll
Reveal a lot about a country's soul.

A small grove massacred to the last ash,
An oak with heart-rot, give away the show:
This great society is going smash;
They cannot fool us with how fast they go,
How much they cost each other and the gods.
A culture is no better than its woods.

THE APPLE ORCHARD

Come just after the sun has gone down, watch
This deepening of green in the evening sward:
Is it not as if we'd long since garnered
And stored within ourselves a something which

From feeling and from feeling recollected,
From new hope and half forgotten joys,
And from an inner dark infused with these,
Issues in thoughts as ripe as windfalls scattered

Here under trees like trees in a Dürer woodcut –
Pendent, pruned, the husbandry of years
Gravid in them until the fruit appears –
Ready to serve, replete with patience, rooted

In the knowledge that no matter how above
Measure or expectation, all must be
Harvested and yielded, when a long life willingly
Cleaves to what's willed and grows in mute resolve.

116 RAINER MARIA RILKE (1875–1926)
TRANSLATED BY SEAMUS HEANEY

ORCHARD

I saw the first pear
as it fell –
the honey-seeking, golden-banded,
the yellow swarm
was not more fleet than I,
(spare us from loveliness)
and I fell prostrate
crying:
you have flayed us
with your blossoms,
spare us the beauty
of fruit-trees.

The honey-seeking
paused not,
the air thundered their song,
and I alone was prostrate.

O rough-hewn
god of the orchard,
I bring you an offering –
do you, alone unbeautiful,
son of the god,
spare us from loveliness:

these fallen hazel-nuts,
stripped late of their green sheaths,
grapes, red-purple,
their berries
dripping with wine,
pomegranates already broken,
and shrunken figs
and quinces untouched,
I bring you as offering.

WILD ORCHARD

It is a broken country,
the rugged land is
green from end to end;
the autumn has not come.

Embanked above the orchard
the hillside is a wall
of motionless green trees,
the grass is green and red.

Five days the bare sky
has stood there day and night.
No bird, no sound.
Between the trees

stillness
and the early morning light.
The apple trees
are laden down with fruit.

Among blue leaves
the apples green and red
upon one tree stand out
most enshrined.

Still, ripe, heavy,
spherical and close,
they mark the hillside.
It is a formal grandeur,

a stateliness,
a signal of finality
and perfect ease.
Among the savage

aristocracy of rocks
one, risen as a tree,
has turned
from his repose.

YOUNG ORCHARD

These trees came to stay.
Planted at intervals of
Thirty feet each way,

Each one stands alone
Where it is to live and die.
Still, when they have grown

To full size, these trees
Will blend their crowns, and hum with
Mediating bees.

Meanwhile, see how they
Rise against their rootedness
On a gusty day,

Nodding one and all
To one another, as they
Rise again and fall,

Swept by flutterings
So that they appear a great
Consort of sweet strings.

RICHARD WILBUR (1921–2017)   121

AFTER APPLE-PICKING

My long two-pointed ladder's sticking through a tree
Toward heaven still,
And there's a barrel that I didn't fill
Beside it, and there may be two or three
Apples I didn't pick upon some bough.
But I am done with apple-picking now.
Essence of winter sleep is on the night,
The scent of apples: I am drowsing off.
I cannot rub the strangeness from my sight
I got from looking through a pane of glass
I skimmed this morning from the drinking trough
And held against the world of hoary grass.
It melted, and I let it fall and break.
But I was well
Upon my way to sleep before it fell,
And I could tell
What form my dreaming was about to take.
Magnified apples appear and disappear,
Stem end and blossom end,
And every fleck of russet showing clear.
My instep arch not only keeps the ache,
It keeps the pressure of a ladder-round.
I feel the ladder sway as the boughs bend.
And I keep hearing from the cellar bin
The rumbling sound

Of load on load of apples coming in.
For I have had too much
Of apple-picking: I am overtired
Of the great harvest I myself desired.
There were ten thousand thousand fruit to touch,
Cherish in hand, lift down, and not let fall.
For all
That struck the earth,
No matter if not bruised or spiked with stubble,
Went surely to the cider-apple heap
As of no worth.
One can see what will trouble
This sleep of mine, whatever sleep it is.
Were he not gone,
The woodchuck could say whether it's like his
Long sleep, as I describe its coming on,
Or just some human sleep.

ORCHARD

Here they stand, a living tree next to a dead one
and a sick tree next to one with sweet fruit,
and none of them knows what happened.
And all of them together, not like human beings
who are separated from one another.

And there is a tree that holds onto the earth with its
      roots
as if with despairing fingers, so the earth won't sink
      down,
and beside it a tree pulled down by the same earth,
and both are one height, you can't tell the difference.

And a wild pigeon cries out a wild hope,
and the whirr of quail in their low flight
brings tidings of things I don't want to know.

And there are mounds of stones for remembrance
and hedges of stones for forgetting,
that's how I mark the boundary between the plots of
      my life,
and that's how the stones will be scattered again over
      the field.

O bliss of the earth swept out to sea in winter
freed of roots and the dead.
O holy erosion that makes us forget.

The cassia gives off its fragrance, and the fragrance
gives back the cassia. That's how imagination
turns a great wheel in my life,
a wheel that won't stop.

Soon my son will rebel against me
even before I am able to tell him
what to do, what path to take.

But peace returns to my heart.
Not peace as it used to be
before it left me years ago. It went away to school,
matured as I did,
and came back looking like me.

YEHUDA AMICHAI (1924–2000)
TRANSLATED BY CHANA BLOCH
AND STEPHEN MITCHELL

THE GREEN ROADS

The green roads that end in the forest
Are strewn with white goose feathers this June,

Like marks left behind by some one gone to the forest
To show his track. But he has never come back.

Down each green road a cottage looks at the forest.
Round one the nettle towers; two are bathed in
    flowers.

An old man along the green road to the forest
Strays from me, from another a child alone.

In the thicket bordering the forest,
All day long a thrush twiddles his song.

It is old, but the trees are young in the forest,
All but one like a castle keep, in the middle deep.

That oak saw the ages pass in the forest:
They were a host, but their memories are lost,

For the tree is dead: all things forget the forest
Excepting perhaps me, when now I see

The old man, the child, the goose feathers at the edge
    of the forest,
And hear all day long the thrush repeat his song.

HOPKINS FOREST

I'd gone out
to get water from the well near the trees,
and was in the presence of another sky.
Gone were the constellations
of a moment before.
Three fourths of the firmament was empty,
the intensest black shone there alone,
though to the left, above the horizon,
in among the tops of the oaks,
was a mass of reddening stars
like firecoals, from which smoke even rose.

I went back inside
and re-opened the book on the table.
Page after page
there were only indecipherable signs,
clusters of forms without any sense,
although vaguely recurring,
and beneath them an abyssal white
as if what we call the spirit
were falling there, soundlessly,
like snow.
Still, I went on turning the pages.

Many years earlier,
in a train at the moment when the day rises,
between Princeton Junction and Newark,
– that is to say, two chance places for me,
two arrows fallen out of nowhere –
the passengers were reading, silent
in the snow that was sweeping the gray windows,
and suddenly,
in a newspaper open next to me –
a big photograph of Baudelaire,
a whole page,
as if the sky were emptying at the world's end
in recognition of the chaos of words.

I put together this dream and this memory
when I walked out, all of one fall,
in woods where snow would soon triumph,
among the many signs we receive,
contradictorily,
from the world devastated by language.
The conflict between two principles,
it seemed to me, was nearing an end,
two lights were becoming one,
the lips of a wound closing.
The white mass of the cold was falling in gusts
on color, but a roof in the distance, a painted
board, standing against a gate,

was color still, and mysterious,
like someone coming out of a tomb, laughing,
and telling the world, "No, don't touch me."

Truly I owe a lot to Hopkins Forest.
I keep it on my horizon, in that place
where the visible gives way to the invisible
in the trembling of the blue in the distance.
I listen to it, amid other sounds,
and at times even, in summer,
kicking the dead leaves of other years
lying as if lit in the shade of oaks
grown densely among stones,
I stop: I believe that the ground is opening
to the infinite, that the leaves are falling into it
without hurry, or coming up again,
above and below no longer existing,
or sound, only the light
whispering of snowflakes that soon
multiply, draw closer, bind together –
and then I see again the whole other sky,
I enter for a moment the great snow.

YVES BONNEFOY (1923–2016)   129
TRANSLATED BY PASCALE TORRACINTA
AND HARRY THOMAS

THE GUM FOREST

After the last gapped wire on a post,
homecoming for me, to enter the gum forest.

This old slow battlefield: parings of armour,
cracked collars, elbows, scattered on the ground.

New trees step out of old: lemon and ochre
splitting out of grey everywhere, in the gum forest.

In there for miles, shade track and ironbark slope,
depth casually beginning all around, at a little
    distance.

Sky sifting, and always a hint of smoke in the light;
you can never reach the heart of the gum forest.

In here is like a great yacht harbour, charmed to
    leaves,
innumerable tackle, poles wrapped in spattered sail,
or an unknown army in reserve for centuries.

Flooded-gums on creek ground, each tall because
    of each.
Now a blackbutt in bloom is showering with bees
but warm blood sleeps in the middle of the day.

The witching hour is noon in the gum forest.
Foliage builds like a layering splash: ground water
drily upheld in edge-on, wax-rolled, gall-puckered
leaves upon leaves. The shoal life of parrots up there.

Stone footings, trunk-shattered. Non-human lights.
Enormous abandoned machines. The mysteries of the
    gum forest.

Delight to me, though, at the water-smuggling creeks,
health to me, too, under banksia candles and combs.

A wind is up, rubbing limbs above the bullock roads;
mountains are waves in the ocean of the gum forest.

I go my way, looking back sometimes, looking
    round me;
singed oils clear my mind, and the pouring sound
    high up.

Why have I denied the passions of my time? To see
lightning strike upward out of the gum forest.

LES MURRAY (1938–2019)   131

SPRING POOLS

These pools that, though in forests, still reflect
The total sky almost without defect,
And like the flowers beside them, chill and shiver,
Will like the flowers beside them soon be gone,
And yet not out by any brook or river,
But up by roots to bring dark foliage on.

The trees that have it in their pent-up buds
To darken nature and be summer woods —
Let them think twice before they use their powers
To blot out and drink up and sweep away
These flowery waters and these watery flowers
From snow that melted only yesterday.

FROM TREES

ORANGE BUDS BY MAIL FROM FLORIDA

*(Voltaire closed a famous argument by claiming that a
ship of war and the grand opera were proofs enough of
civilization's and France's progress, in his day.)*

A lesser proof than old Voltaire's, yet greater,
Proof of this present time, and thee, thy broad
    expanse, America,
To my plain Northern hut, in outside clouds and
    snow,
Brought safely for a thousand miles o'er land and tide,
Some three days since on their own soil live-
    sprouting,
Now here their sweetness through my room
    unfolding,
A bunch of orange buds by mail from Florida.

LOGS ON THE HEARTH
A Memory of a Sister

The fire advances along the log
    Of the tree we felled,
Which bloomed and bore striped apples by the peck
  Till its last hour of bearing knelled.

The fork that first my hand would reach
    And then my foot
In climbings upward inch by inch, lies now
  Sawn, sapless, darkening with soot.

Where the bark chars is where, one year,
    It was pruned, and bled –
Then overgrew the wound. But now, at last,
  Its growings all have stagnated.

My fellow-climber rises dim
    From her chilly grave –
Just as she was, her foot near mine on the bending
    limb,
  Laughing, her young brown hand awave.

December 1915

TREE-BURIAL

Near our southwestern border, when a child
Dies in the cabin of an Indian wife,
She makes its funeral-couch of delicate furs,
Blankets and bark, and binds it to the bough
Of some broad branching tree with leathern thongs
And sinews of the deer. A mother once
Wrought at this tender task, and murmured thus:

  "Child of my love, I do not lay thee down
Among the chilly clods where never comes
The pleasant sunshine. There the greedy wolf
Might break into thy grave and tear thee thence,
And I should sorrow all my life. I make
Thy burial-place here, where the light of day
Shines round thee, and the airs that play among
The boughs shall rock thee. Here the morning sun,
Which woke thee once from sleep to smile on me,
Shall beam upon thy bed and sweetly here
Shall lie the red light of the evening clouds
Which called thee once to slumber. Here the stars
Shall look upon thee – the bright stars of heaven
Which thou didst wonder at. Here too the birds,
Whose music thou didst love, shall sing to thee,
And near thee build their nests and rear their young
With none to scare them. Here the woodland flowers
Whose opening in the spring-time thou didst greet

With shouts of joy, and which so well became
Thy pretty hands when thou didst gather them,
Shall spot the ground below thy little bed.

"Yet haply thou hast fairer flowers than these,
Which, in the land of souls, thy spirit plucks
In fields that wither not, amid the throng
Of joyous children, like thyself, who went
Before thee to that brighter world and sport
Eternally beneath its cloudless skies.
Sport with them, dear, dear child, until I come
To dwell with thee, and thou, beholding me,
From far, shalt run and leap into my arms,
And I shall clasp thee as I clasped thee here
While living, oh most beautiful and sweet,
Of children, now more passing beautiful,
If that can be, with eyes like summer stars –
A light that death can never quench again.

"And now, oh wind, that here among the leaves
Dost softly rustle, breathe thou ever thus
Gently, and put not forth thy strength to tear
The branches and let fall their precious load,
A prey to foxes. Thou, too, ancient sun,
Beneath whose eye the seasons come and go,
And generations rise and pass away,
While thou dost never change – oh, call not up
With thy strong heats, the dark, grim thunder-cloud,
To smite this tree with bolts of fire, and rend

Its trunk and strew the earth with splintered boughs.
Ye rains, fall softly on the couch that holds
My darling. There the panther's spotted hide
Shall turn aside the shower; and be it long,
Long after thou and I have met again,
Ere summer wind or winter rain shall waste
This couch and all that now remains of thee,
To me thy mother. Meantime, while I live,
With each returning sunrise I shall seem
To see thy waking smile, and I shall weep;
And when the sun is setting I shall think
How, as I watched thee, o'er thy sleepy eyes
Drooped the smooth lids, and laid on the round cheek
Their lashes, and my tears will flow again;
And often, at those moments, I shall seem
To hear again the sweetly prattled name
Which thou didst call me by, and it will haunt
My home till I depart to be with thee."

AN ENCOUNTER

Once on the kind of day called "weather breeder,"
When the heat slowly hazes and the sun
By its own power seems to be undone,
I was half boring through, half climbing through
A swamp of cedar. Choked with oil of cedar
And scurf of plants, and weary and over-heated,
And sorry I ever left the road I knew,
I paused and rested on a sort of hook
That had me by the coat as good as seated,
And since there was no other way to look,
Looked up toward heaven, and there against the blue,
Stood over me a resurrected tree,
A tree that had been down and raised again –
A barkless specter. He had halted too,
As if for fear of treading upon me.
I saw the strange position of his hands –
Up at his shoulders, dragging yellow strands
Of wire with something in it from men to men.
"You here?" I said. "Where aren't you nowadays?
And what's the news you carry – if you know?
And tell me where you're off for – Montreal?
Me? I'm not off for anywhere at all.
Sometimes I wander out of beaten ways
Half looking for the orchid Calypso."

THE WOOD-PILE

Out walking in the frozen swamp one gray day,
I paused and said, "I will turn back from here.
No, I will go on farther – and we shall see."
The hard snow held me, save where now and then
One foot went through. The view was all in lines
Straight up and down of tall slim trees
Too much alike to mark or name a place by
So as to say for certain I was here
Or somewhere else: I was just far from home.
A small bird flew before me. He was careful
To put a tree between us when he lighted,
And say no word to tell me who he was
Who was so foolish as to think what *he* thought.
He thought that I was after him for a feather –
The white one in his tail; like one who takes
Everything said as personal to himself.
One flight out sideways would have undeceived him.
And then there was a pile of wood for which
I forgot him and let his little fear
Carry him off the way I might have gone,
Without so much as wishing him good-night.
He went behind it to make his last stand.
It was a cord of maple, cut and split
And piled – and measured, four by four by eight.
And not another like it could I see.

No runner tracks in this year's snow looped near it.
And it was older sure than this year's cutting,
Or even last year's or the year's before.
The wood was gray and the bark warping off it
And the pile somewhat sunken. Clematis
Had wound strings round and round it like a bundle.
What held it though on one side was a tree
Still growing, and on one a stake and prop,
These latter about to fall. I thought that only
Someone who lived in turning to fresh tasks
Could so forget his handiwork on which
He spent himself, the labor of his ax,
And leave it there far from a useful fireplace
To warm the frozen swamp as best it could
With the slow smokeless burning of decay.

BURNING THE CHRISTMAS GREENS

Their time past, pulled down
cracked and flung to the fire
– go up in a roar

All recognition lost, burnt clean
clean in the flame, the green
dispersed, a living red,
flame red, red as blood wakes
on the ash –

and ebbs to a steady burning
the rekindled bed become
a landscape of flame

At the winter's midnight
we went to the trees, the coarse
holly, the balsam and
the hemlock for their green

At the thick of the dark
the moment of the cold's
deepest plunge we brought branches
cut from the green trees

to fill our need, and over
doorways, about paper Christmas
bells covered with tinfoil
and fastened by red ribbons

we stuck the green prongs
in the windows hung
woven wreaths and above pictures
the living green. On the

mantle we built a green forest
and among those hemlock
sprays put a herd of small
white deer as if they

were walking there. All this!
and it seemed gentle and good
to us. Their time past,
relief! The room bare. We

stuffed the dead grate
with them upon the half burnt out
log's smoldering eye, opening
red and closing under them

and we stood there looking down.
Green is a solace

a promise of peace, a fort
against the cold (though we

did not say so) a challenge
above the snow's
hard shell. Green (we might
have said) that, where

small birds hide and dodge
and lift their plaintive
rallying cries, blocks for them
and knocks down

the unseeing bullets of
the storm. Green spruce boughs
pulled down by a weight of
snow – Transformed!

Violence leaped and appeared.
Recreant! roared to life
as the flame rose through and
our eyes recoiled from it.

In the jagged flames green
to red, instant and alive. Green!
those sure abutments ... Gone!
lost to mind

and quick in the contracting
tunnel of the grate
appeared a world! Black
mountains, black and red – as

yet uncolored – and ash white,
an infant landscape of shimmering
ash and flame and we, in
that instant, lost,

breathless to be witnesses,
as if we stood
ourselves refreshed among
the shining fauna of that fire.

IN THE TREE HOUSE AT NIGHT

And now the green household is dark.
The half-moon completely is shining
On the earth-lighted tops of the trees.
To be dead, a house must be still.
The floor and the walls wave me slowly;
I am deep in them over my head.
The needles and pine cones about me

Are full of small birds at their roundest,
Their fists without mercy gripping
Hard down through the tree to the roots
To sing back at light when they feel it.
We lie here like angels in bodies,
My brothers and I, one dead,
The other asleep from much living,

In mid-air huddled beside me.
Dark climbed to us here as we climbed
Up the nails I have hammered all day
Through the sprained, comic rungs of the ladder
Of broom handles, crate slats, and laths
Foot by foot up the trunk to the branches
Where we came out at last over lakes

Of leaves, of fields disencumbered of earth
That move with the moves of the spirit.
Each nail that sustains us I set here;
Each nail in the house is now steadied
By my dead brother's huge, freckled hand.
Through the years, he has pointed his hammer
Up into these limbs, and told us

That we must ascend, and all lie here.
Step after step he has brought me,
Embracing the trunk as his body,
Shaking its limbs with my heartbeat,
Till the pine cones danced without wind
And fell from the branches like apples.
In the arm-slender forks of our dwelling

I breathe my live brother's light hair.
The blanket around us becomes
As solid as stone, and it sways.
With all my heart, I close
The blue, timeless eye of my mind.
Wind springs, as my dead brother smiles
And touches the tree at the root;

A shudder of joy runs up
The trunk; the needles tingle;
One bird uncontrollably cries.
The wind changes round, and I stir
Within another's life. Whose life?
Who is dead? Whose presence is living?
When may I fall strangely to earth,

Who am nailed to this branch by a spirit?
Can two bodies make up a third?
To sing, must I feel the world's light?
My green, graceful bones fill the air
With sleeping birds. Alone, alone
And with them I move gently.
I move at the heart of the world.

IN THE BEECH

I was a lookout posted and forgotten.

On one side under me, the concrete road.
On the other, the bullocks' covert,
the breath and plaster of a drinking place
where the school-leaver discovered peace
to touch himself in the reek of churned-up mud.

And the tree itself a strangeness and a comfort,
as much a column as a bole. The very ivy
puzzled its milk-tooth frills and tapers
over the grain: was it bark or masonry?

I watched the red-brick chimney rear
its stamen course by course,
and the steeplejacks up there at their antics
like flies against the mountain.

I felt the tanks' advance beginning
at the cynosure of the growth rings,
then winced at their imperium refreshed
in each powdered bolt mark on the concrete.
And the pilot with his goggles back came in
so low I could see the cockpit rivets.

My hidebound boundary tree. My tree of knowledge.
My thick-tapped, soft-fledged, airy listening post.

TO PRESERVE FIGS
for Iseult

Go up the whitewashed ladder, by the wall,
        And you'll find seven pounds
    Of them, half-ripened, on the tree.
        The rest were low
    I picked before. They wallowed free
        Near to the ground's
Welter of nettles, apples, weeds. I know,
    You'll have to take care. You might fall.

But there are plenty, seven pounds I'd say,
        Still floundering heavy, green
    And solid in the August air,
        And you can reach
    Them if you climb. So go up there
        And get them, keen
As fig-juice in your envy. Gather each
    Into your fingers, let none stay,

On the branch. It makes a metaphor for lust,
        This grasping for the rounds
    Of unripe figs that ooze their juice,
        Their sperm. It burns,
    That juice, and has no helpful use.
        You'll live with mounds

Of severed energy, with jaded urns
    Whose milked white necks you'll have to trust

Through all your life. It's best you learn that soon.
        The acid in the fruit
    Prickles the world with its pain
        And nothing breaks
    The dour addiction of the brain
        To what may suit,
Or spoil. So watch your mother while she makes
    These tractable. Take up a spoon

And help. Three times they boil, and have to steep,
        Then boil again. Three times
    It always has to be. So let
        Them dry in trays
    In your burning oven. Go and get
        A sugary slime's
Blandishing oil. In winter, black to your gaze,
    Like whales from arctic ice, they'll leap.

GEORGE MacBETH (1932–92)   153

THE TREE THAT BECAME A HOUSE

They came to live in me
who never lived in the woods before.

They kindled a fire
in my roots and branches,
held out their hands
never cramped by the weight of an axe.

The flames lighted a clearing
in the dark overhead, a sky of wood;
they burned in me a little hollow
like a moon of ash.

I stand here fastened in a living box,
half in my dream life
with finches, wind and fog –

an endless swaying,
divided in the walls that keep them,
in the floors that hold them up,
in the sills they lean upon.

The children look out in wonder
at trees shouldering
black against the starlight;
they speak in whispers,
searching the forest of sleep.

My split heart creaks in the night
around them,
my dead cones drop in silence.

JOHN HAINES (1924–2011)

PINE NEEDLES

   some raindrops still clinging
– I brought you these pine boughs

– you look like you'd jump up
& put your hot cheek against this green,
fiercely thrust your cheek
into the blue pine needles
greedily
– you're going to startle the others –
did you want to go to the woods

                     that much?
burning with fever
tormented by sweat and pain

And me working happily in the sunlight
Thinking of you, walking slowly through the trees
    "Oh I'm all right now
    it's like you brought the
    center of the forest right here ..."

Like a bird or a squirrel
you long for the woods.
how you must envy me,
my sister, who this very day must
    travel terribly far.
can you manage it alone?
        ask me to go with you
            crying – ask me –
your cheeks however
how beautiful they are.

I'll put these fresh pine boughs
on top of the mosquito net
they may drip a little
ah, a clean
smell like turpentine.

THE TREE

It looked like oak, white oak, oak of the oceans,
oak of the Lord, live oak, oak if a boy could choose.
The names, like ganglia, were the leaves, flesh

of our fathers. So Sundays I would stand
on a chair and trace, as on a county map,
back to the beginnings of cousins,

nomenclature. This branch, this root . . .
I could feel the weight of my body take hold,
toe in. I could see the same shape in my hand.

And if from the floor it looked like a cauliflower,
dried, dusted, pieced back together, paper –
my bad eyes awed by the detailed dead and named –

it was the stalk of the spine as it culminates at
        the brain,
a drawing I had seen in a book about the body,
        each leaf
inlaid until the man's whole back, root and stem,
        was veins.

TREE SURGEONS

Like feelers off into last night's dream, out beyond
    the screens,
they move in approximate circles around my
    neighbor's elm.
Gleeful performers,
they know they belong here,

drawing their large bows, toothed strings,
across each branch with great discrimination.
What crooked instruments! And yet
symmetry governs,

theirs an elm of two nests, two squirrels,
a skinny elm of split decisions.
How evenly it is rid of itself, tree of no nuance,
    no preference,
of no cardinals loading red

onto the sunny half. My neighbor sweeps the porch.
It is taking longer than expected.
There is no *temporarily* she thinks.
I think she secretly admires the dust, how evenly
    each grain

falls into place, as if grown upward
from the meaning of the thing itself – davenport,
    commode –
more even than forgiveness,
better even than the clean slate of *you were only*
    dreaming.

The tree is almost done.
Offspring to mainline, now everything is sure where
    it began.
My window splits in two –
her elm, then mine, shaggy,

headed some other way.
Like one who leaves, and the other who remains,
    they are
each other's constant, sullen victims
and yet safe

from one another.
The daylight has gone although we are not yet in
    darkness.
I stand at my window. The light draws in.
I cannot say why, but they are much too safe from
    one another.

160 JORIE GRAHAM (1950–)

GLADNESS GONE

From THE BOOK OF JOEL

Be confounded, O tillers of the soil,
    wail, O vinedressers,
for the wheat and the barley;
    because the harvest of the field
        has perished.

The vine withers,
    the fig tree languishes.
Pomegranate, palm, and apple,
    all the trees of the field are
        withered;
and gladness fails
    from the sons of men.

THE POPLAR-FIELD

The Poplars are fell'd, farewell to the shade
And the whispering sound of the cool colonnade,
The winds play no longer and sing in the leaves,
Nor Ouse on his bosom their image receives.

Twelve years have elapsed since I last took a view
Of my favourite field and the bank where they grew,
And now in the grass behold they are laid,
And the tree is my seat that once lent me a shade.

The black-bird has fled to another retreat
Where the hazels afford him a screen from the heat,
And the scene where his melody charm'd me before,
Resounds with his sweet-flowing ditty no more.

My fugitive years are all hasting away,
And I must e'er long lie as lowly as they,
With a turf on my breast and a stone at my head
E'er another such grove shall arise in its stead.

'Tis a sight to engage me if any thing can
To muse on the perishing pleasures of Man;
Though his life be a dream, his enjoyments, I see,
Have a Being less durable even than he.

164 WILLIAM COWPER (1731–1800)

THROWING A TREE

New Forest

The two executioners stalk along over the knolls,
Bearing two axes with heavy heads shining and
  wide,
And a long limp two-handled saw toothed for
  cutting great boles,
And so they approach the proud tree that bears the
  death-mark on its side.

Jackets doffed they swing axes and chop away just
  above ground,
And the chips fly about and lie white on the moss
  and fallen leaves;
Till a broad deep gash in the bark is hewn all the
  way round,
And one of them tries to hook upward a rope, which at
  last he achieves.

The saw then begins, till the top of the tall giant
  shivers:
The shivers are seen to grow greater each cut than
  before:
They edge out the saw, tug the rope; but the tree
  only quivers,

And kneeling and sawing again, they step back to try
   pulling once more.

   Then, lastly, the living mast sways, further sways:
      with a shout
   Job and Ike rush aside. Reached the end of its long
      staying powers
   The tree crashes downward: it shakes all its
      neighbours throughout,
And two hundred years' steady growth has been
   ended in less than two hours.

I saw them like beavers or insects gnawing at the trunk of this noble tree, the diminutive manikins with their crosscut saw which could scarcely span it. ... I watch closely to see when it begins to move. Now the sawyers stop, and with an axe open it a little on the side toward which it leans, that it may break the faster. And now their saw goes again. Now surely it is going; it is inclined one quarter of the quadrant, and, breathless, I expect its crashing fall. But no, I was mistaken; it has not moved an inch; it stands at the same angle as at first. It is fifteen minutes yet to its fall. Still its branches wave in the wind, as if it were destined to stand for a century, and the wind soughs through its needles as of yore; it is still a forest tree, the most majestic tree that waves over Musketaquid. The silvery sheen of the sunlight is reflected from its needles; it still affords an inaccessible crotch for the squirrel's nest; not a lichen has forsaken its mast-like stem.

Now, now's the moment! The manikins at its base are fleeing from their crime. They have dropped the guilty saw and axe. How slowly and majestically it starts! As if it were only swayed by a summer breeze, and would return without a sigh to its location in the air. And now it fans the hillside with its fall, and it lies down to its bed in the valley, from which it is never to rise, as softly as a feather, folding its green mantle about it like a warrior, as if, tired of standing, it embraced the earth with silent joy, returning its elements to the dust again. But hark! there you only saw, but did not hear. There now comes up a deafening crash to these rocks, advertising you that even trees do not die without a groan. It rushes to embrace the earth, and mingle its elements with the dust. And now all is still once more and forever, both to eye and ear.

Its gracefully spreading top was a perfect wreck on the hillside as if it had been made of glass, and the tender cones of one year's growth upon its summit appealed in vain and too late to the mercy of the chopper. The space it occupied in upper air is vacant for the next two centuries. It is lumber. He has laid waste the air. When the fish hawk in the spring revisits the banks of the Musketaquid, he will circle in vain to find his accustomed perch, and the hen-hawk will mourn for the pines lofty enough to protect her brood. A plant which it has taken two centuries to perfect, rising by slow stages into the heavens, has this afternoon ceased to exist. Its sapling top had expanded to this January thaw as the forerunner of summers to come. Why does not the village bell sound a knell? I hear no knell tolled, see no procession of mourners in the streets, or the woodland aisles. The squirrel has leaped to another tree; the hawk has circled further off, and has now settled upon a new aerie, but the woodman is preparing to lay his axe at the root of that also.

BINSEY POPLARS

felled 1879

My aspens dear, whose airy cages quelled,
Quelled or quenched in leaves the leaping sun,
All felled, felled, are all felled;
    Of a fresh and following folded rank
            Not spared, not one
            That dandled a sandalled
      Shadow that swam or sank
On meadow and river and wind-wandering weed-
    winding bank.

O if we but knew what we do
      When we delve or hew –
  Hack and rack the growing green!
      Since country is so tender
  To touch, her being só slender,
  That, like this sleek and seeing ball
  But a prick will make no eye at all,
  Where we, even where we mean

To mend her we end her,
When we hew or delve:
After-comers cannot guess the beauty been.
Ten or twelve, only ten or twelve
Strokes of havoc únselve
The sweet especial scene,
Rural scene, a rural scene,
Sweet especial rural scene.

AT BINSEY

clouds growing
in beauty

at end of day
a white rack

of two parallel
vertebrated

spines
the trembling

aspens felled
rank after

rank of bole
& leaf as if

an eyeball
had been sliced

THE POPLAR AND THE PASSER-BY

They're widening the street
Clogged with traffic
They're felling the poplars

The bulldozers take a run-up
And with a single blow
Knock down the trees

One poplar just trembled
Withstood the iron

The bulldozer pulls back
From her noisily
Prepares for the final charge

In the huddle of passers-by
There's an elderly man

He takes his hat off to the poplar
Waves his umbrella at her
And shouts at the top of his voice

Don't give in love

VASKO POPA (1922–91)
TRANSLATED BY ANNE PENNINGTON

THE TREES ARE DOWN

— and he cried with a loud voice:
Hurt not the earth, neither the sea, nor the trees —
(Revelation)

They are cutting down the great plane-trees at the
      end of the gardens.
For days there has been the grate of the saw, the swish
      of the branches as they fall,
The crash of trunks, the rustle of trodden leaves,
With the "Whoops" and the "Whoas," the loud
      common talk, the loud common laughs of
      the men, above it all.

I remember one evening of a long past Spring
Turning in at a gate, getting out of a cart, and finding
      a large dead rat in the mud of the drive.
I remember thinking: alive or dead, a rat was a god-
      forsaken thing,
But at least, in May, that even a rat should be alive.

The week's work here is as good as done. There is just
      one bough
  On the roped bole, in the fine gray rain,
    Green and high
    And lonely against the sky.
      (Down now! —)

And but for that,
    If an old dead rat
Did once, for a moment, unmake the Spring, I might
        never have thought of him again.

It is not for a moment the Spring is unmade today;
These were great trees, it was in them from root to
        stem:
When the men with the "Whoops" and the "Whoas"
        have carted the whole of the whispering
        loveliness away
Half the Spring, for me, will have gone with them.

It is going now, and my heart has been struck with the
        hearts of the planes;
Half my life it has beat with these, in the sun, in the
        rains,
    In the March wind, the May breeze,
In the great gales that came over to them across the
        roofs from the great seas.
    There was only a quiet rain when they were
        dying;
    They must have heard the sparrows flying,
And the small creeping creatures in the earth where
        they were lying –
    But I, all day, I heard an angel crying:
        "Hurt not the trees."

CHARLOTTE MEW (1869–1928)   175

CLEARANCES, VIII

I thought of walking round and round a space
Utterly empty, utterly a source
Where the decked chestnut tree had lost its place
In our front hedge above the wallflowers.
The white chips jumped and jumped and skited high.
I heard the hatchet's differentiated
Accurate cut, the crack, the sigh
And collapse of what luxuriated
Through the shocked tips and wreckage of it all.
Deep-planted and long gone, my coeval
Chestnut from a jam jar in a hole,
Its heft and hush become a bright nowhere,
A soul ramifying and forever
Silent, beyond silence listened for.

TO A FALLEN ELM

Old Elm that murmured in our chimney top
The sweetest anthem autumn ever made
And into mellow whispering calms would drop
When showers fell on thy many colored shade
And when dark tempests mimic thunder made
While darkness came as it would strangle light
With the black tempest of a winter night
That rocked thee like a cradle to thy root
How did I love to hear the winds upbraid
Thy strength without while all within was mute
It seasoned comfort to our hearts desire
We felt thy kind protection like a friend
And pitched our chairs up closer to the fire
Enjoying comforts that was never penned

Old favourite tree thoust seen times changes lower
But change till now did never come to thee
For time beheld thee as his sacred dower
And nature claimed thee her domestic tree
Storms came and shook thee with a living power
Yet stedfast to thy home thy roots hath been
Summers of thirst parched round thy homely bower
Till earth grew iron – still thy leaves was green
The children sought thee in thy summer shade
And made their play house rings of sticks and stone

The mavis sang and felt himself alone
While in thy leaves his early nest was made
And I did feel his happiness mine own
Nought heeding that our friendship was betrayed

Friend not inanimate – tho stocks and stones
There are and many cloathed in flesh and bones
Thou ownd a language by which hearts are stirred
Deeper than by the atribute of words
Thine spoke a feeling known in every tongue
Language of pity and the force of wrong
What cant asumes what hypocrites may dare
Speaks home to truth and shows it what they are

I see a picture that thy fate displays
And learn a lesson from thy destiny
Self interest saw thee stand in freedoms ways
So thy old shadow must a tyrant be
Thoust heard the knave abusing those in power
Bawl freedom loud and then oppress the free
Thoust sheltered hypocrites in many a shower
That when in power would never shelter thee
Thoust heard the knave supply his canting powers
With wrongs illusions when he wanted friends
That bawled for shelter when he lived in showers
And when clouds vanished made thy shade amends

With axe at root he felled thee to the ground
And barked of freedom – O I hate that sound

It grows the cant terms of enslaving tools
To wrong another by the name of right
It grows a liscence with oer bearing fools
To cheat plain honesty by force of might
Thus came enclosure – ruin was her guide
But freedoms clapping hands enjoyed the sight
Tho comforts cottage soon was thrust aside
And workhouse prisons raised upon the scite
Een natures dwelling far away from men
The common heath became the spoilers prey
The rabbit had not where to make his den
And labours only cow was drove away
No matter – wrong was right and right was wrong
And freedoms brawl was sanction to the song

Such was thy ruin music making Elm
The rights of freedom was to injure thine
As thou wert served so would they overwhelm
In freedoms name the little that is mine
And these are knaves that brawl for better laws
And cant of tyranny in stronger powers
Who glut their vile unsatiated maws
And freedoms birthright from the weak devours

JOHN CLARE (1793–1864)   179

ELMS

All morning the tree men have been taking down the
    stricken elms skirting the broad sidewalks.
The pitiless electric chain saws whine tirelessly up and
    down their piercing, operatic scales
and the diesel choppers in the street shredding the
    debris chug feverishly, incessantly,
packing truckload after truckload with the feathery,
    homogenized, inert remains of heartwood,
twig and leaf and soon the block is stripped, it is as
    though illusions of reality were stripped:
the rows of naked facing buildings stare and think,
    their divagations more urgent than they were.
"The winds of time," they think, the mystery charged
    with fearful clarity: "The winds of time ..."
All afternoon, on to the unhealing evening, minds
    racing, "Insolent, unconscionable, the winds of
    time ..."

PANEGYRIC FOR THE PLANE TREE
FALLEN ON FIFTH AVENUE

At the end of Eighty-eighth,
across from the museum and as west as east
will take you to the park from Gracie Mansion.
Before the lightning brought it down,
before it fell at evening rush hour,
before another summer burned the money
off its leaves, before
it put a sudden stop to double lanes of traffic,
you could stand here late at night
in the middle of the street
and watch it grow,
the outer darker skin
flaking to the bone bark underneath.
It was probably too tall,
and filled too easily with wind,
too brilliantly with rain
and ice and snow.
And probably its roots were shallow
with the sidewalk, the breakable
high branches threatening.
Maybe it was thirty, thirty-five years old,
planted in the forties, after war,
and because of where it was,
flowering like a blessing,

allowed its larger seasons.
In 1979, sempiternal and a year,
the city was a buyer's market,
if you already owned
and had a million in the bank.
Mornings the gold coin of the sun
rose from the East River, set in the Hudson.
These hybrids of the sycamore
lined all the avenue along the park.
If a tree falls in the forest . . .
If a tree has no witness . . .
A hundred of us saw it hit and fall.
Fall slow enough no one near was caught.
First the thunderbolt thrown straight
at its carved heart, then
the killing blood-spurt of a fire.
It was cut up and gone within an hour.
How many times I leaned against its length
waiting for the crossing light to change.

ODE TO A FALLEN CHESTNUT

From the bristling foliage
you fell
complete
all polished wood,
shining mahogany,
at the ready
like a violin which has just
been born up there
and drops
emprisoned treasures,
a hidden sweetness
perfected in secret
among birds and leaves,
the school of form,
lineage of kindling and flour,
an oval instrument
preserving in its structure
virgin delight, an edible rose.
Up there you left behind
the hedgehog husk
half opening its barbs
in the tree's twilight –
through that division
witnessed the world:
birds

brimming with syllables,
star-spangled
dew,
and below,
the heads of boys
and girls,
the restless waving grass,
smoke without ceiling.
You made up your mind
and jumped to earth,
tanned and prepared,
firm and soft
like a teenage breast
of the American islands.
You fell
thwacking
the ground
yet nothing changed –
grass
went on waving, the old
chestnut tree kept whispering with the mouths
of a whole grove of trees,
red autumn lost a leaf,
the steady hours kept busy at their work
throughout the earth.
Because
you're hardly more

than just a seed:
chestnut tree, autumn, earth,
water, sky, silence
mellowed the germ,
the floury thickness,
the maternal eyelids
which, buried, will open again
on to the sky
an artless majesty
of foliage,
the damp conspiracy
of new roots,
the old and new dimensions
of another chestnut tree pegged in earth.

PABLO NERUDA (1904–73)

TRANSLATED BY NATHANIEL TARN

SONNET XVIII
(Second series)

And change with hurried hand has swept these scenes:
The woods have fallen, across the meadow-lot
The hunter's trail and trap-path is forgot,
And fire has drunk the swamps of evergreens;
Yet for a moment let my fancy plant
These autumn hills again: the wild dove's haunt,
The wild deer's walk. In golden umbrage shut,
The Indian river runs, Quonecktacut!
Here, but a lifetime back, where falls tonight
Behind the curtained pane a sheltered light
On buds of rose or vase of violet
Aloft upon the marble mantel set,
Here in the forest-heart, hung blackening
The wolfbait on the bush beside the spring.

FIFTY FAGGOTS

There they stand, on their ends, the fifty faggots
That once were underwood of hazel and ash
In Jenny Pinks's Copse. Now, by the hedge
Close packed, they make a thicket fancy alone
Can creep through with the mouse and wren.
    Next spring
A blackbird or a robin will nest there,
Accustomed to them, thinking they will remain
Whatever is for ever to a bird:
This Spring it is too late; the swift has come.
'Twas a hot day for carrying them up:
Better they will never warm me, though they must
Light several Winters' fires. Before they are done
The war will have ended, many other things
Have ended, maybe, that I can no more
Foresee or more control than robin and wren.

EDWARD THOMAS (1878–1917)   187

I WAS SLEEPING WHERE THE BLACK OAKS MOVE

We watched from the house
as the river grew, helpless
and terrible in its unfamiliar body.
Wrestling everything into it,
the water wrapped around trees
until their life-hold was broken.
They went down, one by one,
and the river dragged off their covering.

Nests of the herons, roots washed to bones,
snags of soaked bark on the shoreline:
a whole forest pulled through the teeth
of the spillway. Trees surfacing
singly, where the river poured off
into arteries for fields below the reservation.

When at last it was over, the long removal,
they had all become the same dry wood.
We walked among them, the branches
whitening in the raw sun.
Above us drifted herons,
alone, hoarse-voiced, broken,
settling their beaks among the hollows.

Grandpa said, *These are the ghosts of the tree people,*
moving above us, unable to take their rest.

Sometimes now, we dream our way back to the heron
      dance.
Their long wings are bending the air
into circles through which they fall.
They rise again in shifting wheels.
How long must we live in the broken figures
their necks make, narrowing the sky.

LOUISE ERDRICH (1955–)

SONNET XI
(Second series)

Still pressing through these weeping solitudes,
Perchance I snatch a beam of comfort bright
And pause to fix the gleam or lose it quite
That darkens as I move or but intrudes
To baffle and forelay: as sometimes here,
When late at night the waried engineer
Driving his engine up through Whately woods
Sees on the track a glimmering lantern light
And checks his crashing speed, with hasty hand
Reversing and retarding; – but again,
Look where it burns, a furlong on before!
The witchlight of the reedy rivershore,
The pilot of the forest and the fen,
Not to be left, but with the waste woodland.

THE WAR AGAINST THE TREES

The man who sold his lawn to standard oil
Joked with his neighbors come to watch the show
While the bulldozers, drunk with gasoline,
Tested the virtue of the soil
Under the branchy sky
By overthrowing first the privet-row.

Forsythia-forays and hydrangea-raids
Were but preliminaries to a war
Against the great-grandfathers of the town,
So freshly lopped and maimed.
They struck and struck again,
And with each elm a century went down.

All day the hireling engines charged the trees,
Subverting them by hacking underground
In grub-dominions, where dark summer's mole
Rampages through his halls,
Till a northern seizure shook
Those crowns, forcing the giants to their knees.

I saw the ghosts of children at their games
Racing beyond their childhood in the shade,
And while the green world turned its death-foxed
        page

And a red wagon wheeled,
I watched them disappear
Into the suburbs of their grievous age.

Ripped from the craters much too big for hearts
The club-roots bared their amputated coils,
Raw gorgons matted blind, whose pocks and scars
Cried Moon! on a corner lot
One witness-moment, caught
In the rear-view mirrors of the passing cars.

MANGROVE

I saw its periscope in the tide;
its torpedo-seed seeking the soft side
of the island, the grey mud-bank.
And, where it touched, it seemed the land sank
with its trees exploding from water; the green
mangroves' fountainhead of leaves bursting, seen
like a mushroom-top of detritus and spray.
Today, in my boat, at the close end of the bay,
I saw its dark devastations; islet and spit
sunk in the flat high tide. Where these war-seeds hit,
gaps of horizon and sea; then trees ... gaps ... trees
... like men on a flushed foredeck. No ease:
the drab olive-green swarming everywhere;
troops of the mangroves, uniform, everywhere.

JOHN BLIGHT (1913–95)

WHEN THERE WERE TREES

I can remember when there were trees,
great tribes of spruces who deckled themselves
    in light,
beeches buckled in pewter, meeting like Quakers,
the golden birch, all cutwork satin,
courtesan of the mountains; the paper birch
trying all summer to take off its clothes
like the swaddlings of the newborn.

The hands of a sassafras blessed me.
I saw maples fanning the fire in their stars,
heard the coins of the aspens rattling like teeth,
saw cherry trees spraying fountains of light,
smelled the wine my heel pressed from ripe apples,
saw a thousand planets bobbing like bells
on the sleeve of the sycamore, chestnut, and lime.

The ancients knew that a tree is worthy of worship.
A few wise men from their tribes broke through
    the sky,
climbing past worlds to come and the rising moon
on the patient body of the tree of life,
and brought back the souls of the newly slain,
no bigger than apples, and dressed the tree
as one of themselves and danced.

Even the conquerors of this country
lifted their eyes and found the trees
more comely than gold: *Bright green trees,*
and whole land so green it is pleasure to look on it
and the greatest wonder to see the diversity.
During that time, I walked among trees,
the most beautiful things I had ever seen.

Watching the shadows of trees, I made peace with
    mine.
Their forked darkness gave motion to morning light.
Every night the world fell to the shadows,
and every morning came home, the dogwood floating
its petals like moons on a river of air,
the oak kneeling in wood sorrel and fern,
the willow washing its hair in the stream.

And I saw how the logs from the mill floated
downstream, saw otters and turtles that rode them,
and though I heard the saws whine in the woods
I never thought men were stronger than trees.
I never thought those tribes would join their brothers,
the buffalo and the whale, the leopard, the seal,
    the wolf,
and the men of this country who knew how to sing
    them.

Nothing I ever saw washed off the sins of the world
so well as the first snow dropping on trees.
We shoveled the pond clear and skated under their
    branches,
our voices muffled in their huge silence.
The trees were always listening to something else.
They didn't hear the beetle with the hollow tooth
grubbing for riches, gnawing for empires, for gold.

Already the trees are a myth,
half gods, half giants in whom nobody believes.
But I am the oldest woman on earth,
and I can remember when there were trees.

"THE GROVES ARE DOWN"

The groves are down
          cut down
Groves of Ahab, of Cybele
Pine trees, knobbed twigs
    thick cone and seed
    Cybele's tree this, sacred in groves
Pine of Seami, cedar of Haida
Cut down by the prophets of Israel
    the fairies of Athens
    the thugs of Rome
        both ancient and modern;
Cut down to make room for the suburbs
Bulldozed by Luther and Weyerhaeuser
Crosscut and chainsaw
    squareheads and finns
    high-lead and cat-skidding
Trees down
Creeks choked, trout killed, roads.

Sawmill temples of Jehovah.
Squat black burners 100 feet high
Sending the smoke of our burnt
Live sap and leaf
To his eager nose.

GARY SNYDER (1930–)

LYRICS,
MEDITATIONS

TREES IN THE GARDEN

Ah in the thunder air
how still the trees are!

And the lime tree, lovely and tall, every leaf silent
hardly looses even a last breath of perfume.

And the ghostly, creamy coloured little tree of leaves
white, ivory white among the rambling greens,
how evanescent, variegated elder, she hesitates on the
    green grass
as if, in another moment, she would disappear
with all her grace of foam!

And the larch that is only a column, it goes up too tall
    to see:
and the balsam pines that are blue with the grey-blue
    blueness of things from the sea,
and the young copper beech, its leaves red-rosy at
    the ends,
how still they are together, they stand so still
in the thunder air, all strangers to one another
as the green grass glows upwards, strangers in
    the garden.

D. H. LAWRENCE (1885–1930)   201

BIRCHES

When I see birches bend to left and right
Across the line of straighter darker trees,
I like to think some boy's been swinging them.
But swinging doesn't bend them down to stay.
Ice-storms do that. Often you must have seen them
Loaded with ice a sunny winter morning
After a rain. They click upon themselves
As the breeze rises, and turn many-colored
As the stir cracks and crazes their enamel.
Soon the sun's warmth makes them shed crystal shells
Shattering and avalanching on the snow-crust –
Such heaps of broken glass to sweep away
You'd think the inner dome of heaven had fallen.
They are dragged to the withered bracken by the load,
And they seem not to break; though once they
    are bowed
So low for long, they never right themselves:
You may see their trunks arching in the woods
Years afterwards, trailing their leaves on the ground
Like girls on hands and knees that throw their hair
Before them over their heads to dry in the sun.
But I was going to say when Truth broke in
With all her matter-of-fact about the ice-storm
I should prefer to have some boy bend them
As he went out and in to fetch the cows –

Some boy too far from town to learn baseball,
Whose only play was what he found himself,
Summer or winter, and could play alone.
One by one he subdued his father's trees
By riding them down over and over again
Until he took the stiffness out of them,
And not one but hung limp, not one was left
For him to conquer. He learned all there was
To learn about not launching out too soon
And so not carrying the tree away
Clear to the ground. He always kept his poise
To the top branches, climbing carefully
With the same pains you use to fill a cup
Up to the brim, and even above the brim.
Then he flung outward, feet first, with a swish,
Kicking his way down through the air to the ground.
So was I once myself a swinger of birches;
And so I dream of going back to be.
It's when I'm weary of considerations,
And life is too much like a pathless wood
Where your face burns and tickles with the cobwebs
Broken across it, and one eye is weeping
From a twig's having lashed across it open.
I'd like to get away from earth awhile
And then come back to it and begin over.

May no fate willfully misunderstand me
And half grant what I wish and snatch me away
Not to return. Earth's the right place for love:
I don't know where it's likely to go better.
I'd like to go by climbing a birch tree,
And climb black branches up a snow-white trunk
Toward heaven, till the tree could bear no more,
But dipped its top and set me down again.
That would be good both going and coming back.
One could do worse than be a swinger of birches.

THE CEDARS

The dried body of winter is hard to kill.
Frost crumbles the dead bracken, greys the old grass,
and the great hemisphere of air goes flying
barren and cold from desert or polar seas
tattering fern and leaf. By the sunken pool
the sullen sodom-apple grips his scarlet fruit.

Spring, returner, knocker at the iron gates,
why should you return? None wish to live again.
Locked in our mourning, in our sluggish age,
we stand and think of past springs, of deceits not yet
        forgotten.
Then we answered you in youth and joy; we threw
open our strongholds and hung our walls with
        flowers.
Do not ask us to answer again as then we answered.

For it is anguish to be reborn and reborn:
at every return of the overmastering season
to shed our lives in pain, to waken into the cold,
to become naked, while with unbearable effort
we make way for the new sap that burns along old
        channels –
while out of our life's substance, the inmost of our
        being,

form those brief flowers, those sacrifices, soon falling,
which spring the returner demands, and demands
 for ever.

Easier, far easier, to stand with downturned eyes
and hands hanging, to let age and mourning cover us
with their dark rest, heavy like death, like the ground
from which we issued and towards which we crumble.
Easier to be one with the impotent body of winter,
and let our old leaves rattle on the wind's currents –
to stand like the rung trees whose boughs no longer
 murmur
their foolish answers to spring; whose blossoms
 now are
the only lasting flowers, the creeping lichens of death.

Spring, impatient, thunderer at the doors of iron,
we have no songs left. Let our boughs be silent.
Hold back your fires that would sear us into flower
 again,
and your insistent bees, the messengers of generation.
Our bodies are as old as winter and would remain in
 winter.
So the old trees plead, clinging to the edge of darkness.
But round their roots the mintbush makes its buds
 ready,

and the snake in hiding feels the sunlight's finger.
The snake, the fang of summer, beauty's double
     meaning,
shifts his slow coils and feels his springtime hunger.

ON TREES
Secular Metamorphosis of Joyce Kilmer's "Trees"

Don't talk to me about trees having branches and roots:
they are all root, except for the trunk, and the high
    root,
waving its colors in the air, is no less snarled in its food
than is the low root snarled in its specialty: nourishment
in dirt. What with the reciprocal fair trade of the trunk
holding the two roots together and apart in equipoise,
the whole tree stands in solid connection to its
    whole self
except for the expendable beauty of its seasonal ends,
and is so snarled at either end in its contrary goods
that it studs the dirt to the air with its living wood.
This anagogic significance grows with its growth
    for years,
twigging in all directions as an evidence of entirety,
although it waves back and forth in the wind and is
    a host
to fungi, insects, men, birds, and the law of entropy.

SOME TREES

These are amazing: each
Joining a neighbour, as though speech
Were a still performance.
Arranging by chance

To meet as far this morning
From the world as agreeing
With it, you and I
Are suddenly what the trees try

To tell us we are:
That their merely being there
Means something; that soon
We may touch, love, explain.

And glad not to have invented
Such comeliness, we are surrounded:
A silence already filled with noises,
A canvas on which emerges

A chorus of smiles, a winter morning.
Placed in a puzzling light, and moving,
Our days put on such reticence
These accents seem their own defence.

JOHN ASHBERY (1927–2017)   209

TREE AT MY WINDOW

Tree at my window, window tree,
My sash is lowered when night comes on;
But let there never be curtain drawn
Between you and me.

Vague dream-head lifted out of the ground,
And thing next most diffuse to cloud,
Not all your light tongues talking aloud
Could be profound.

But, tree, I have seen you taken and tossed,
And if you have seen me when I slept,
You have seen me when I was taken and swept
And all but lost.

That day she put our heads together,
Fate had her imagination about her,
Your head so much concerned with outer,
Mine with inner, weather.

SUPPOSE NO TREES STOOD NEAR MY WINDOW

Suppose no trees stood near my window –
Those managing to look straight down into me –
Then my heart, obeying its own fierce laws,
Would long ago have given up.

My being after death is the one inside the tall willow,
Inside the somber cypress that knows me,
Who feels sad that I am in the world,
And who does not understand why I remain here
    so long.

JULES SUPERVIELLE (1884–1966)
TRANSLATED BY ROBERT BLY

WINTER TREES
for Jan Susina

To watch snow sift into woods is to
Feel yourself growing gently toward death,
Yet it is trees that teach us how to live.
In some places a person can exist
For many years without seeing a tree:
That must be the way of anger and despair.
Better to have the constant example
Of their patience and perfection,
To witness the blossoming and decay,
Watch snow resolve itself through branches,
Gathering softly at the nodes and shag.
Better to somehow join them and become
Part of the last stand in the world.

INTO THE TREE

And he placed at the east of the garden of Eden Cherubim,
and a flaming sword which turned every way, to keep the
way to the tree of life. — GENESIS 3, 24

And he looked up and said, "I see men as trees, walking."
— MARK 8, 24

The tree, says good Swedenborg, is a close relative
    of man.
Its boughs like arms join in an embrace.
The trees in truth are our parents,
We sprang from the oak, or perhaps, as the Greeks
    maintain, from the ash.

Our lips and tongue savor the fruit of the tree.
A woman's breast is called apple or pomegranate.
We love the womb as the tree loves the dark womb of
    the earth.
Thus, what is most desirable resides in a single tree,
And wisdom tries to touch its coarse-grained bark.

I learned, says the servant of the New Jerusalem,
That Adam in the garden, i.e., mankind's Golden Age,
Signifies the generations after the pre-adamites
Who are unjustly scorned though they were gentle,

Kind to each other, savage yet not bestial,
Happy in a land of fruits and springwaters.

Adam created in the image and in the likeness
Represents the parting of clouds covering the mind.
And Eve, why is she taken from Adam's rib?
– Because the rib is close to the heart, that's the name
    of self-love,
And Adam comes to know Eve, loving himself in her.

Above those two, the tree. A huge shade tree.

Of which the counselor of the Royal Mining Commission says the following in his book *De amore conjugiali:*

"The Tree of Life signifies a man who lives from God, or God living in man; and as love and wisdom, or charity and faith, or good and truth, make the life of God in man, these are signified by the Tree of Life, and hence the eternal life of the man. ... But the tree of science signifies the man who believes that he lives from himself and not from God; thus that love and wisdom, or charity and faith, or good and truth, are in man from himself and not from God; and he believes this because he thinks and wills, and speaks and acts, in all likeness and appearance as from himself."

Self-love offered the apple and the Golden Age was
    over.
After it, the Silver Age, the Bronze Age. And the Iron.

Then a child opens its eyes and sees a tree for the first
    time.
And people seem to us like walking trees.

CZESLAW MILOSZ (1911–2004)   215
TRANSLATED BY CZESLAW MILOSZ
AND ROBERT HASS

UNDER THE OAK

You, if you were sensible,
When I tell you the stars flash signals, each one
    dreadful,
You would not turn and answer me
"The night is wonderful."

Even you, if you knew
How this darkness soaks me through and through,
    and infuses
Unholy fear in my essence, you would pause to
    distinguish
What hurts from what amuses.

For I tell you
Beneath this powerful tree, my whole soul's fluid
Oozes away from me as a sacrifice steam
At the knife of a Druid.

Again I tell you, I bleed, I am bound with withies,
My life runs out.
I tell you my blood runs out on the floor of this oak,
Gout upon gout.

Above me springs the blood-born mistletoe
In the shady smoke.
But who are you, twittering to and fro
Beneath the oak?

What thing better are you, what worse?
What have you to do with the mysteries
Of this ancient place, of my ancient curse?
What place have you in my histories?

D. H. LAWRENCE (1885–1930)   217

GHAZAL

The soul of summer gone – tall hillside trees
Invite the failing sun, amber, despair.

What is it they lose? Their great, luxurious spread?
The dew-drenched coldmass, shapeliness, at dawn?

The Sibyl's sibilance at noon? Night nestings
And the rapacious loneliness of owls at rest?

I think of their hooded eyes and the harsh faith
Of inner chambers, the pulse of a drowsing tree.

Who sits there waiting in a corner like a mind
Dreaming bit by bit, a heap of thinking rags?

Leaves everywhere, and the terror of leaves
Mounded and drifting, too beautiful to bear!

THESE GREEN-GOING-TO-YELLOW

This year,
I'm raising the emotional ante,
putting my face
in the leaves to be stepped on,
seeing myself among them, that is;
that is, likening
leaf-vein to artery, leaf to flesh,
the passage of a leaf in autumn
to the passage of autumn,
branch-tip and winter spaces
to possibilities, and possibility
to God. Even on East 61st Street
in the blowzy city of New York,
someone has planted a gingko
because it has leaves like fans like hands,
hand-leaves, and sex. Those lovely
Chinese hands on the sidewalks
so far from delicacy
or even, perhaps, another gender of gingko –
do we see them?
No one ever treated us so gently
as these green-going-to-yellow hands
fanned out where we walk.
No one ever fell down so quietly
and lay where we would look

when we were tired or embarrassed,
or so bowed down by humanity
that we had to watch out lest our shoes stumble,
and looked down not to look up
until something looked like parts of people
where we were walking. We have no
experience to make us see the gingko
or any other tree,
and, in our admiration for whatever grows tall
and outlives us,
we look away, or look at the middles of things,
which would not be our way
if we truly thought we were gods.

220 MARVIN BELL (1937–)

CHRISTMAS TREE

★

To be
Brought down at last
From the cold sighing mountain
Where I and the others
Had been fed, looked after, kept still,
Meant, I knew – of course I knew –
That it would be only a matter of weeks,
That there was nothing more to do.
Warmly they took me in, made much of me,
The point from the start was to keep my spirits up.
I could assent to that. For honestly,
It did help to be wound in jewels, to send
Their colors flashing forth from vents in the deep
Fragrant sables that cloaked me head to foot.
Over me then they wove a spell of shining –
Purple and silver chains, eavesdripping tinsel,
Amulets, milagros: software of silver,
A heart, a little girl, a Model T,
Two staring eyes. Then angels, trumpets, BUD and
BEA
(The children's names) in clownlike capitals,
Somewhere a music box whose tiny song
Played and replayed I ended before long
By loving. And in shadow behind me, a primitive IV

To keep the show going. Yes, yes, what lay ahead
Was clear: the stripping, the cold street, my chemicals
Plowed back into the Earth for lives to come –
No doubt a blessing, a harvest, but one that doesn't
bear,
Now or ever, dwelling upon. To have grown so thin.
Needles and bone. The little boy's hands meeting
About my spine. The mother's voice: *Holding up
wonderfully!*
No dread. No bitterness. The end beginning. Today's
Dusk room aglow
For the last time
With candlelight.
Faces love-lit,
Gifts underfoot.
Still to be so poised, so
Receptive. Still to recall, to praise.

LEARNING THE TREES

Before you can learn the trees, you have to learn
The language of the trees. That's done indoors,
Out of a book, which now you think of it
Is one of the transformations of a tree.

The words themselves are a delight to learn,
You might be in a foreign land of terms
Like samara, capsule, drupe, legume and pome,
Where bark is papery, plated, warty or smooth.

But best of all are the words that shape the leaves –
Orbicular, cordate, cleft and reniform –
And their venation-palmate and parallel –
And tips – acute, truncate, auriculate.

Sufficiently provided, you may now
Go forth to the forests and the shady streets
To see how the chaos of experience
Answers to catalogue and category.

Confusedly. The leaves of a single tree
May differ among themselves more than they do
From other species, so you have to find,
All blandly says the book, "an average leaf."

Example, the catalpa in the book
Sprays out its leaves in whorls of three
Around the stem; the one in front of you
But rarely does, or somewhat, or almost;

Maybe it's not catalpa? Dreadful doubt.
It may be weeks before you see an elm
Fanlike in form, a spruce that pyramids,
A sweetgum spiring up in steeple shape.

Still, *pedetemtim* as Lucretius says,
Little by little, you do start to learn;
And learn as well, maybe, what language does
And how it does it, cutting across the world

Not always at the joints, competing with
Experience while cooperating with
Experience, and keeping an obstinate
Intransigence, uncanny, of its own.

Think finally about the secret will
Pretending obedience to Nature, but
Invidiously distinguishing everywhere,
Dividing up the world to conquer it,

And think also how funny knowledge is:
You may succeed in learning many trees
And calling off their names as you go by,
But their comprehensive silence stays the same.

AN ELM TREE
in memory of Albert Herrick

The winter birds have come;
One of them knows my name:
    Chick-a-dee-dee-dee-dee-dee.
Now, a whole pack of them

Skinning past like hoods;
Up in the maples, hidden,
    One shuffles his deck of wings
And deals me a word, a word;

Then, like a struck spark, gone.
Yet, there's my sentence again
    From an oak branch overhead;
Another one, farther on

Jeers me behind the barn
Where the old path turns
    Past the smoldering mound
Where years of rubbish burn,

And out beyond to the grove
Of pine trees, chill as the grave,
    Where the sun's light never falls
But needles, steady as grief,

Sift up, muffling and soft,
The lower limbs crack off,
    And you sink halfway to the knee
In what shone green, aloft,

What will seep down and in
Before it sees light again.
    You *could* stop, but the bird
Says your name, then

You come out into the whole
Light of day on the hill
    Where, on the high cleared brow
Strongly arching still

Stands that blighted elm,
Rawboned, overwhelmed,
    Stripped like the old mad king
Of this vegetable realm.

This was your great-uncle's tree
That he watered every day –
    30 buckets and the spring
Half a mile away.

The leaves gone and the bark.
As if a man stood, stark,
　　Till all had fallen away
But the nerves' field thrown on the dark

Woods behind his back.
A small boy, you came to the shack
　　Where he lived alone on his land;
You felt ashamed and sick

At the dark, heavy stain
On your thin wrist all day
　　After he shook your hand.
May that not wash away.

MY FATHER AS A MAPLE TREE

As large as a one-
footed elephant,
its several trunks

and tusks,
bent landward, leafed
and petaled.

And in its hundred, two-
hundred years of age,
bowed not by kneeling

on that leg
but by the troubling
weight of wind

and its own heavy,
splintered crown,
while a great palmetto ear,

like a burned-out sponge,
lay on the ground.
That's how he looked

this morning –
a thrashing, fissured
monument pecked

by birds that nominate
his skin, a boundary
tree, cleaved

by lightning, lost
to what it bound.

"Jesus Christ,"
a neighbor urged,
"cut it down."

MICHAEL COLLIER (1953–)   229

TREE MARRIAGE

In Chota Nagpur and Bengal
the betrothed are tied with threads to
mango trees, they marry the trees
as well as one another, and
the two trees marry each other.
Could we do that some time with oaks
or beeches? This gossamer we
hold each other with, this web
of love and habit is not enough.
In mistrust of heavier ties,
I would like tree-siblings for us,
standing together somewhere, two
trees married with us, lightly, their
fingers barely touching in sleep,
our threads invisible but holding.

THE CEMETERY OF ORANGE TREES IN CRETE

In Crete the old orange trees are cut back until they
    are stumps,
with little leaves coming out again from the butchered
    arms.
They are painted white and stand there in long
    straight rows
like the white gravestones at Gettysburg and
    Manassas.
    I first came across them on the bus ride to Omalos
as we began our climb through the empty mountains,
thinking of the beauty and exhaustion that lay ahead.
They are mementos of my journey south, the renewal
of my youth, green leaves growing out of my neck,
my shoulders flowering again with small blossoms,
my body painted white, my hands joining
the other hands on the hill, my white heart
    remembering
the violence and sorrow that gave us our life again.

IN CALIFORNIA DURING THE GULF WAR

Among the blight-killed eucalypts, among
trees and bushes rusted by Christmas frosts,
the yards and hillsides exhausted by five years of
    drought,

certain airy white blossoms punctually
reappeared, and dense clusters of pale pink, dark
    pink –
a delicate abundance. They seemed

like guests arriving joyfully on the accustomed
festival day, unaware of the year's events, not
    perceiving
the sackcloth others were wearing.

To some of us, the dejected landscape consorted well
with our shame and bitterness. Skies ever-blue,
daily sunshine, disgusted us like smile-buttons.

Yet the blossoms, clinging to thin branches
more lightly than birds alert for flight,
lifted the sunken heart

even against its will.
                    But not
as symbols of hope: they were flimsy
as our resistance to the crimes committed

– again, again – in our name; and yes, they return,
year after year, and yes, they briefly shone with serene
        joy
over against the dark glare

of evil days. They *are*, and their presence
is quietness ineffable – and the bombings *are*, were,
no doubt will be; that quiet, that huge cacophany

simultaneous. No promise was being accorded, the
        blossoms
were not doves, there was no rainbow. And when it
        was claimed
the war had ended, it had not ended.

THE WILLOW

The willow
Over past the potato patch
Is the least lucky
Of all the trees of our village –
The spot has been turned into a rubbish dump.

Yes. In the first place, no one knows whose it was,
Who planted it there, or why –
We don't know.
If it's always clean and tidy as a peasant's hut
Round other
Perfectly ordinary, pleasant willows,
Round that godforsaken one
All manner of trash is piled.
People bring scrap iron,
Galoshes, boots,
Not fit for anything now, of course,
(If they were any good at all, they wouldn't be there),
And when the cat dies, it's dumped by the tree.
So encircled is the poor willow
With old boots, rags and rotting cats
That it's advisable to give it a wide berth.

But still, when May comes,
The willow, up to its knees in muck,
Suddenly begins gently to gild itself.
It doesn't give a damn about the torn galoshes,
The jars and tins, the old clothes.
It blossoms as do all its earthly sisters.
Shyly it blossoms
With innocent flowers, so pure,
Turned towards the sun, for the first time opening.
And the sun shines. And the whole tree smells
    of honey.

And, incidentally, bees fly to it,
In spite of the rubbish lying at its foot,
And bear away the translucent honey of its flowers
To people who abuse trees.

VLADIMIR SOLOUKHIN (1924–97)   235
TRANSLATED BY DANIEL WEISSBORT

SEQUOIA

Gothic spires of needles in the valley of a stream
not far from Mount Tamalpais where morning and
      evening
dense fog breathes the elation or rage of the ocean

on display in this reservation of giants a cross-section
      of a tree the coppery stump of the West
with vast concentric rings like ripples on water
on which some cross-grained fool has carved the dates
      of history
an inch from the center Nero looks down at burning
      Rome
farther out the battle of Hastings the longboats
      moving in darkness
the panic of the Saxons the death of the ill-starred
      Harold
all laid bare by a pair of compasses
and finally nearing the coast of the bark the
      Normandy landing

the Tacitus of this stump was a geometer he had no
      adjectives
he lacked the grammar of havoc he didn't know words
and so he counted added
years and centuries as if to say there is nothing
nothing beyond birth and death just birth and death
and between them
the bleeding pulp of the sequoia

ZBIGNIEW HERBERT (1924–98)   237
TRANSLATED BY JACK NIECKO AND
ROBERT MEZEY

SEMPERVIRENS IN WINTER

Those lumpish mounds of dead leaves
huddled along the back fence are the blackberries
that overran the yard – five of us took all day
with hoe and shovel
gloves and machete

cutting them back last spring
to plant this garden and look: everything is puddles
and dissolution – borders breached, eroded beds,
the bean-row furrows
obliterated.

The tree stump in the middle
is old growth redwood cut knee high last century.
Its upper branches shaded all this ground and now
its broad girth serves
as garden altar:

the rain slick surface glistens
pocked by the downpour pooling in the weathered
        grooves
of its annual rings. Each year it sprouts back
another chaplet
of sapling shoots.

THE TREES

The trees are coming into leaf
Like something almost being said;
The recent buds relax and spread,
Their greenness is a kind of grief.

Is it that they are born again
And we grow old? No, they die too.
Their yearly trick of looking new
Is written down in rings of grain.

Yet still the unresting castles thresh
In fullgrown thickness every May.
Last year is dead, they seem to say,
Begin afresh, afresh, afresh.

PHILLIP LARKIN (1922–85)   239

TO A BLOSSOMING PEAR TREE

Beautiful natural blossoms,
Pure delicate body,
You stand without trembling.
Little mist of fallen starlight,
Perfect, beyond my reach,
How I envy you.
For if you could only listen,
I would tell you something,
Something human.

An old man
Appeared to me once
In the unendurable snow.
He had a singe of white
Beard on his face.
He paused on a street in Minneapolis
And stroked my face.
Give it to me, he begged.
I'll pay you anything.

I flinched. Both terrified,
We slunk away,
Each in his own way dodging
The cruel darts of the cold.

Beautiful natural blossoms,
How could you possibly
Worry or bother or care
About the ashamed, hopeless
Old man? He was so near death
He was willing to take
Any love he could get,
Even at the risk
Of some mocking policeman
Or some cute young wiseacre
Smashing his dentures,
Perhaps leading him on
To a dark place and there
Kicking him in his dead groin
Just for the fun of it.

Young tree, unburdened
By anything but your beautiful natural blossoms
And dew, the dark
Blood in my body drags me
Down with my brother.

THE WIDOW'S LAMENT IN SPRINGTIME

Sorrow is my own yard
where the new grass
flames as it has flamed
often before but not
with the cold fire
that closes round me this year.
Thirtyfive years
I lived with my husband.
The plumtree is white today
with masses of flowers.
Masses of flowers
load the cherry branches
and color some bushes
yellow and some red
but the grief in my heart
is stronger than they
for though they were my joy
formerly, today I notice them
and turned away forgetting.
Today my son told me
that in the meadows,
at the edge of the heavy woods
in the distance, he saw
trees of white flowers.

I feel that I would like
to go there
and fall into those flowers
and sink into the marsh near them.

EVERYBODY'S TREE

The storm broke over us on a summer night,
All brilliance and display; and being out,
Dangerously I thought, on the front porch standing,
Over my head the lightning skated and blistered
And sizzled and skidded and yelled in the bursting
    down
Around my maybe fourteen-years-old being,
And in spite of all the fireworks up above
And what you'd thought would have been the heat
    of all
That exuberant rage, the air was suddenly cool
And fresh and as peaceable as could be,
Down on the porch, so different from what it was
My body was expecting. The raindrops on
The front porch railing arms peacefully dripped
As if they weren't experiencing what
Was coming down from above them as an outrage.
My body could reinterpret it as a blessing,
Being down there in the cool beneath the heat.
It wasn't of course being blessed but being suddenly
Singled out with a sense of being a being.

Sometime early on in the nineteenth century,
Down in the part of New Jersey called New Sweden,
Someone with some familial link to me,

244

Maybe a grandsire down a maternal line,
Whose name was Isaiah Toy, was sitting up
In the house of his dying bachelor uncle, who
Was also Isaiah Toy, and Isaiah Toy,
His uncle, would leave his farm to Isaiah Toy,
His nephew, who was sitting in a chair
In the next room to where his uncle was dying.
I don't know what kind of light it would have been
That he was reading the Bible by while his uncle
Slept toward leaving the farm to him, when suddenly,
Reading, who was it, Matthew, or maybe Mark,
The glory of the Lord broke over his head,
Or so he said. Methodists got excited when
In the woods of their confusion suddenly
The moonlight burst above their heads and they
Were ever after then enlightened beings.
"Light suddenly broke upon his mind. For fear
Of disturbing his dying uncle with his joy,
The expression of which he could not repress, he went
Out of the house into the brilliant moonlight
Shining upon the snow, and gave vent to his feelings,
Shouting 'Glory to God! Glory to God in the
    Highest.'"

Coming back in from the porch, while the storm
     went on
Above our little house, I went to close the window
Of the dining room that looked out back of the house
And I could see, could dimly see, the backs
Of the Bowdoin Street houses all in a row,
Occasionally lit up and washed blank by
Downpours of the lightning of the storm:
The Beckers' house, the Gileses' house, the
     Demarests',
Jean Williams's where she lay in "the sleeping-
     sickness."
And Bessie Phelps's house, the one next to hers,
The property lines of the houses and their yards
Made briefly briefly clear by the lightning flashing.
Running along the back of the hither yards
Was a tiny ditch defining the property lines
Between where our Yale Street backyards ended
And where the yonder Bowdoin Street houses'
     backyards
Backed up to it; my childhood fantasy thought
The waterless tiny ditch was the vestige of
A mysterious long ago bygone vanished river
That came from somewhere else and went somewhere.
I don't know, didn't know, though of course I knew
     them,
Whatever went on in those houses, or in my mind,

Or my mother's mind, or my father's, asleep upstairs,
Though I kept wondering, and wonder still,
What is it they were doing? Who were they?
All, all, are gone, the unfamiliar faces.

Over beyond in the night there was a houseless
Wooded lot next door to Bessie's house;
Because of the houselessness and because of the trees,
I could think of it as a forest like the forest
In Hawthorne's great short story "Young Goodman
     Brown,"
And from out that window looking out at the back
I could faintly see, or thought I could see,
Maybe once or twice, by a flash, a raining gust
Of the light of lightning, the waving tops of trees
In that empty wooded lot beyond Bessie's house.
The houseless tiny lot seemed like a forest
And in the forest there was a certain tree
Which all of us children somehow knew was known
As Everybody's Tree, so it was called,
Though nobody knew who it was who gave it its
     name;
And on the smooth hide of its trunk there were
     initials,
Nobody knew who it was who had inscribed them.
We children had never gathered around that tree
To show each other our bodies.

                                    I remember how
Crossing through that houseless wooded lot,
On my way home on an autumn afternoon,
That strange tree, with the writing on it, seemed
Ancient, a totem, a rhapsody playing a music
Written according to an inscrutable key.
How did I ever know what the tree was called?
Somebody must have told me. I can't remember.
Whoever it was has become a shade imagined
From an ancient unrecoverable past.

ACKNOWLEDGMENTS

Thanks are due to the following copyright holders for permission to reprint:

YEHUDA AMICHAI: "Orchard" from *The Selected Poetry of Yehuda Amichai*, translated from the Hebrew by Chana Bloch and Stephen Mitchell, © 1986, 1996, 2013 by Chana Bloch and Stephen Mitchell. First published by Harper & Row in 1986, first University of California Press edition in 1996. JOHN ASHBERY: "Some Trees" from *Collected Poems: 1956–1987*, Library of America, 2008. Georges Borchardt Agency. W. H. AUDEN: "Woods (Bucolics: II)," copyright 1953 by W. H. Auden, renewed © 1981 by The Estate of W. H. Auden; from *Collected Poems* by W. H. Auden. Used by permission of Random House, an imprint and division of Penguin Random House LLC. All rights reserved. Faber and Faber/Curtis Brown. MATSUO BASHO: "From all these trees", translated by Robert Hass, from *The Essential Haiku*, edited by Robert Hass, The Ecco Press, 1994. GIORGIO BASSANI: "The Racial Laws", translated by Jamie McKendrick, from *Poetry*, April 2007. MARVIN BELL: "These Green-Going-to-Yellow" from *Nightworks: Poems 1962–2000*. Copyright © 1985 by Marvin Bell. Reprinted with the permission of The Permissions Company, LLC on behalf of Copper Canyon Press, www.coppercanyonpress.org. JOHN BLIGHT: "Mangrove" from *Selected Poems: 1939–1990*, University of Queensland Press, Australia. Used with permission. YVES BONNEFOY: "The Apples" from *Beginning and End of the Snow* by Yves Bonnefoy, translated by Emily Grosholz, Copyright © 2012. Used by permission of Rowman & Littlefield Publishing Group. All rights reserved. "Hopkins Forest", translated by Pascale Torracinta and Harry Thomas, from *Threepenny Review*, Summer 2006. Translation copyright © by Harry Thomas and Pascale Torracinta. Reprinted with permission. "Lightning", translated by

from *Poems of the American West*, Alfred A. Knopf, 2002. Original poem published by Cztelnik, Warsaw. HOMER: Excerpts from *The Odyssey* (translated by Robert Fagles) from *The Odyssey*, Penguin Books, 1996. PATRICK KAVANAGH: "Beech Tree", *Collected Poems*, W. W. Norton and Company, 1964. STANLEY KUNITZ: "The War Against the Trees" from *The Poems of Stanley Kunitz 1928-1978*, Little, Brown and Company, 1979. W. W. Norton and Company, *Collected Poems* by Stanley Kunitz, 2002. PHILIP LARKIN: "The Trees" from *The Complete Poems*, edited by Archie Burnett, Farrar, Straus and Giroux and Faber and Faber, 2012. Reprinted with permission. D. H. LAWRENCE: "Trees in the Garden" by D. H. Lawrence, from *The Complete Poems of D. H. Lawrence*, edited by V. De Sola Pinto & F. W. Roberts. Copyright © 1964, 1971 by Angela Ravagli and C. M. Weekly, Executors of the Estate of Frieda Lawrence Ravagli. Used by permission of Viking Penguin, a division of Penguin Books USA Inc. DENISE LEVERTOV: "In California During the Gulf War" by Denise Levertov, from *Evening Train*, copyright © 1992 by Denise Levertov. Reprinted by permission of New Directions Publishing Corp. "The Willows of Massachusetts" by Denise Levertov, from *Poems 1960-1967*, copyright © 1966 by Denise Levertov. Reprinted by permission of New Directions Publishing Corp. GEORGE MACBETH: To Preserve Figs" from *Collected Poems 1958-1982*, Hutchinson, 1989. Sheil Land Associates. ANTONIO MACHADO: "To a Dried-up Elm", translated by Jamie McKendrick, from *Anomaly* by Jamie McKendrick, Faber and Faber. Reprinted with permission. LORENTZOS MAVILIS: "The Olive Tree" (translated by A. E. Stallings) from *The Greek Poets: Homer to the Present*, edited by Peter Constantine, Rachel Hadas, Edmund Keeley and Karen Van Dyck, W. W. Norton and Company, 2010. WILLIAM MEREDITH: "Tree Marriage" is reprinted from *Effort at Speech: New and Selected Poems* by William Meredith, published by TriQuarterly Books/Northwestern University Press in 1997. Copyright © 1997 by William